10 YEARS OF UNPRECEDENTED

PEACE
FAVOR
&
ABUNDANCE

BISHOP STEPHEN A. DAVIS

10 Years of Unprecedented Peace, Favor & Abundance

by Bishop Stephen A. Davis

Trade paperback ISBN: 978-1-943294-35-0
Ebook ISBN: 978-1-943294-36-7

Cover design by Martijn van Tilborgh

10 Years of Unprecedented Peace, Favor & Abundance is also available on Amazon Kindle, Barnes & Noble Nook and Apple iBooks.

Contents

Dedication

I WOULD LIKE TO THANK all of those who have worked to make sure this book was published and released this year. I want to show great gratitude to one of the greatest churches in the Body of Christ, New Birth Birmingham. Thank you! I can never forget the impact my Spiritual father (Apostle Eddie L. Long) has had on my life, pushing me beyond preaching good sermons to publishing great messages. My daughters, Sasha, Amber, and April, have been an extremely great inspiration to me in structuring inner wisdom for the advancement of our public audience. My wife, Michelle Darlene Davis, has not failed in the areas of believing, supporting, encouraging and LOVING me to move in greater dimensions that made this book possible. All the honor and glory goes to my God Most High! THANK YOU!

Foreword

Peace, be still. (Mark 4:29, AKJV)

GOD SAID IT THROUGH HIS son Jesus so many years ago, and he's saying that to so many of us still today. He's presented the command — the gift — of peace. And in this book, Bishop Stephen A. Davis is reminding us that we have the opportunity to walk in peace, favor, and abundance unlike anything we have ever witnessed in our lives before.

Through his plain talk and real-life scenarios, he shows that it is now up to us to take action to bring these gifts into fruition. Accepting that God is providing these for us is one thing. Choosing to actively pursue his gifts is another.

Read on to see what Bishop Davis has to say about the productivity that follows peace. It is part of God's abundance and favor. It's the ability to accomplish great things for the kingdom and in our own lives.

The first step in retrieving God's gifts is believing they exist and are created especially for us. Faith is what God desires from you. We can take a cue from the centurion who had faith enough to know that if Jesus — even from afar — spoke healing on his servant, the servant would be healed. Expectations of abundance. That's what He wants. That's what the bishop is showing us how to walk in throughout this text.

This book is not just for the church leader, but for anyone trying to leave behind a rebellious spirit and find the peace of the Lord on a level that surpasses all understanding.

— Bishop Eddie L. Long

Introduction

Instead of your shame you shall have double honor,
And instead of confusion they shall rejoice in their
portion. Therefore in their land they shall possess double;
Everlasting joy shall be theirs. — Isaiah 61:7

As I received this Word from the Lord about being in a season of unprecedented peace, favor and abundance, I began to rejoice on the inside because I know God is not a man that He should lie, nor the son of man that He would change His mind. For such a time as this, God is showing us that we are not a people who will always be in bondage to a system, any system that teaches us to be limited. In this season of unprecedented peace, favor and abundance, there are no limits! You are a great people with great purpose that is why in this season it is important to be connected, faithful, committed, focused and prepared. I am so grateful to have had the pleasure of writing this book to encourage you to no longer complain or struggle, but to rest in knowing that you are in a season that has never been witnessed before, a season that is unparalleled, a season God has prepared just for you. Let us agree in prayer: Father, I honor you and I bless you for this holy day. I thank you for this holy season and I thank you for being a holy God. Allow my mind to be opened so that the information from these pages will have a phenomenal and positive effect on my life. Thank you for what you are doing in this season of unprecedented peace, favor and abundance. In Jesus' Name, Amen.

— Bishop Stephen A. Davis
Birmingham, Alabama
January, 2014

CHAPTER 1

What Is Unprecedented?

Now it came to pass when the king was dwelling in his house, and the Lord had given him rest from all his enemies all around... — 2 Samuel 7:1 (New King James Version)

The Lord gave them rest all around, according to all that He had sworn to their fathers. And not a man of all their enemies stood against them; the Lord delivered all their enemies into their hand. Not a word failed of any good thing which the Lord had spoken to the house of Israel. All came to pass. — Joshua 21: 44–45 (New King James Version)

VERSE ONE OF 2 SAMUEL chapter 7 uses the word around, meaning everything that was working against King David was no longer working against him.

King David was in a season of rest, a season of peace. There is a statement affirmed through God, my spiritual father (Apostle Eddie L. Long) and other brothers in the ministry, who carry major influence not just in the United States, but in this world, that characterizes this season. This statement that God gave me was "unprecedented peace, favor and abundance."

The word *unprecedented* is defined as "without previous incident, never before known or previously experienced." So, unprecedented peace must mean a peace that surpasses all understanding, the peace that is being brought on the Body of Christ. Unprecedented favor then, means favor never before known or experienced; another word is unparalleled. You will not be able to put anything up against us as the Body of Christ in comparison and determine what we are or what we are going to be. Hence, we are in a season of unprecedented peace.

As a body of true believers, we are not warring with what God said. Let me give you some validation on this because some of us like to stay in a complaining, struggling, drama season. Well, I'm sorry, I work to get paid. I don't know about you, but I work to get paid; if I remain faithful, I have a payday coming. My payday begins now! I don't know about you, but if you are connected to the Body of Christ, to a pastor with vision and purpose, when it is time to get paid for being faithful, committed, focused, you get paid. My pay time begins, now, and it's not going to end during this unprecedented season!

Some of you have been through so much Hell, you don't know how to live in Heaven. You wake up, waiting for a situation to hit instead of waiting on health, wealth and vitality to hit. I expect mighty things to happen in my life every day. You may have had a rough time, but it was preparing you for a new year, a new beginning. I've had some pretty rough years, but I didn't mind going through a rough time to get to my good time. "Behold I set before you an open door, but there are many adversaries," but they're not going to stop me now! I have fought through too much; I have held on too long; I have persevered; I have prayed; I have kept my integrity. How about you?

PREPARE FOR YOUR SEASON

You don't have any faith because you have some error in your beliefs. It's not hard to believe what God said. If you're accustomed to what God says, it's easy. For example, Jesus said, "Rise and walk" and the lame man took up his bed and walked. Jesus operates the same way today. When God says, "Be whole"—you get healed; God says, "You're rich"—poverty leaves you. This move can't be paralleled with any move that's happened before.

Luke 4:13 reads, "**Now** when the devil had ended every temptation, he departed from Him until an opportune time." Jesus was under pressure with temptation but, at the end, Satan, trials, adversities and pressure left Him and they couldn't come back. It doesn't make sense to have a lifetime of pressure when an unprecedented season is prepared for you—now you need to prepare for it. If your parents told you that there is always going to be struggle, that's a lie. There are seasons you are going to enter into when there are not going to be any devils. There are seasons when you can't get depressed; you can't go bankrupt; you can't die. Whatever was bad can't handle me or you, not in this season. You're coming into your season!

I see it all the time, as a Bishop, when I have to accomplish certain things within a certain period of time. It seems like when we are working on a project, some situation hits the life of somebody who's vital to the plan, and it throws them off track. This situation then makes it difficult to accomplish all we could accomplish because someone is going through turbulence. Now, someone who had the reins can't focus on what the agenda is, what the priority is; therefore, you have to put the project on pause. Not in this season! It's too much that we, as the Body of Christ, are called to do; whatever comes your way is not going to throw you off focus. No, you're going to stay the course, remain in this season and stay *focused*.

STAY FOCUSED

It doesn't matter how many enemies come your way; they are not going to be able to stand against you because God needs you focused. Whatever "it" is, it won't throw you off focus. It's just an illusion; it's outside of you; it's not inside of you; it can't destroy you; it can't overthrow you; it can't defeat you. Get out of your personal situation because it's not going to help right now.

When God blesses us, He's blessing all of us. Some people are too selfish and too independent; you want your house, your children, your money blessed, but we want everyone who is connected to be blessed. If I'm trying to get rich and not trying to help you get rich, if I'm getting rich off of you or trying to get ahead of you, then my motives are wrong. Your motives have to be right. If I'm rich, you'll be rich; if I'm healed, you'll be healed; if I'm happy, you might as well get ready to be happy! This is the time to stay focused by staying connected.

ANOTHER LOOK AT UNPRECEDENTED

Since you don't have anything to compare with the season we are in and where God is taking us, just go along for the ride. Don't gossip and criticize your pastor and your brothers and sisters in Christ when you see them begin to prosper and excel. There's no vocabulary for what God is bringing to the Body of Christ. In 1 Chronicles 22:9, King Solomon is the closest example of what we will be accomplishing in this season. David was a man of war, and when God got ready to do the next phase of His plan on the earth, it couldn't be done by someone who couldn't put the plan in place without watching for the enemy. That type of thinking that believes someone is out to get you is not going to work. God has given you rest from war. Get in your unprecedented season!

If you line yourself up, no enemy can stop you. Rest doesn't mean sit in a recliner and watch television; rest means, "I'm going to keep them away from you so you can build what I need you to build in this season of your life." All the resources that were held up are being released on your behalf. Get yourself together because you're coming into your season, and it's a season of plenty; a season of overflow, order and power; a season you've never experienced before in your life—unprecedented. What God is doing for the Body of Christ doesn't make sense; you can't use your mind to even articulate it. It's bigger than you, me and the Body of Christ. Start praising God because it's here. It Is Here!

THE TRUTH AND NOTHING BUT THE TRUTH

I've been talking about truth. The only way you can get the best God has is through truth. The truth of the matter is we haven't had this type of season before because we didn't see what God needed us to see in the scriptures. Wherever there is disorder, there is poverty. This day will start the rest of your life; whatever comes after you generationally will not know struggle. When God calls you to do something extraordinary, He tells you to gather all whom He has chosen.

THE CHOSEN ONES

In 1 Chronicles chapter 23, David gathered the Levites; in chapter 24, he gathered the priests; in chapter 25, he gathered the musicians; in chapter 26, he gathered the gatekeepers and in chapter 27, he gathered the military. When you read your Bible, you have to read your Bible with understanding or you will try to get what you are not a candidate to get. What we have to do is make sure the Levites and priests are in place, because, if we do, we are ready to build. The worshipers are the Levites who create an atmosphere of worship. The worst thing you can do is to try to build on the waste of the previous generation. Most of us only know the generation before us that failed and they failed because they did not seek out the truth.

In order to have integrity, you have to find some Levites and priests; if you take somebody who's supposed to be doing something else and put them in a higher rank as a Levite and priest, they will abandon their assignment when the first temptation comes along. Therefore, we can fortify the house by putting the right people in the right place and then, the next ten years, your money won't be funny and your body won't be sick. You don't have to know their name but you will know "the blessing of the Lord that maketh rich and addeth no sorrow." We are going back to the basics and laying the right foundation (based on the Word of Truth) so that we can have God do what He has called us to do.

GOD HAD AN ORDER

Do you notice that in a family, if a mother and father sing, the children also sing? If they play instruments, the children also play instruments. If it is the same in the music world, it's the same as far as the Levites, priests, gatekeepers and military. You come to the defense of the Bishop because you're a part of the military. That's why fight comes up out of you when the ministry is confronted; you are a warrior, a real warrior, called to stand for the cause. Aaron had two sons who tripped out, but the next couple of sons raised up the entire priesthood; so all the priests came from Aaron. If a mother and father have a child, whatever the call was on the mother and father is on that child and the grandchildren. Our children have gone into the secular world, but they are coming back in this season.

God had an order. You wonder where that passion in you comes from; it comes from your assigned place in the Body of Christ. We have put people in place who didn't have a passion; they just wanted to do something in church. In that day that they were building the temple, they didn't just have people doing something; those people were about to become some of the wealthiest people the world had ever seen. We have to get it right. If we get it right from the front to the back, everyone will be rolling. Back in that day, you didn't have to figure out what someone was going to do. They had the DNA of their parents. When you get it in order, you don't have anything but success. God had a plan before you ever got here, and, if you get in His plan, fall in line, you will be so blessed you won't know what to do with yourself. Whatever was upstream is getting ready to hit your DNA right now.

REST IN THIS SEASON

God says, "Because my agenda is so important, I'm going to give you some rest from everything that's been attacking you and coming against you; I'm going to give you rest because what I want is greater than what you want. I'm going to drive the devil away from you that you couldn't drive away from yourself. I'm going to bring you into a season. I know it's been difficult, I know it's been hard, but I am God. I'm going to bring you into a season because there are some things I need done in the earth realm that can't be done unless you put your hands on it. I have already released the agenda. I've already released the vision." You need to get yourself ready because God is doing it. It's already done. It's already in the earth, and He would never send a vision without provision.

So, you can't understand why the corporate arena doesn't like you because you operate in integrity? The Levite spirit steps up and says, "I don't know why, but I can't do it like this." Then you go home feeling bad about a decision the corporation made about taking advantage of people. But that Levite in you won't let you rest while you are telling lies and doing wrong. You will not be comfortable because you are called to a higher level and your conscience is going to eat you up; but in this season of unprecedented peace, favor and abundance, you are going to find your place, God's chosen place for you.

THESE ARE YOUR YEARS

When we (the Body of Christ) start doing it right, then we'll own everything that is ready to be claimed by us. God is bringing into existence everything He promised. It shall come to pass. Have you ever met someone and it seems like you have known them all your life? They are probably your spiritual relative. You are going to run into some people who will make your baby leap. Why, because you are a musician, a Levite, a gatekeeper, one chosen by God. God didn't save you to do your own thing; He saved you because He has a purpose for your life.

When it talks about the musicians, the Bible says when they began to play, they were prophesying; when they began to play, people began to see their future. In contrast, the church has had paid musicians. It is impossible to meet up with those called to those positions and stay in a lower level. Some of you have been in church so long and haven't seen anything happen that you have no expectation. Look again. Something is about to happen. Something has already happened. These are your years!

Chapter 2

Unprecedented Peace, Favor and Abundance

IN ORDER TO HAVE A better understanding of God's plan for our lives, regarding Peace, Favor and Abundance, we must stay focused on the word *unprecedented*. Remember, we defined unprecedented as "without previous incident, something that you have never experienced before, never known or experienced." We do not have a comparison, and I don't know about you, but I don't have time for more of what I've already experienced. What I've experienced hasn't made me who God has intended for me to be. I need a fresh experience; we all need fresh experiences that stir us up and drive us toward the destiny God designed for us.

Some people think it is just talk. However, I don't ever believe anything God tells me is just talk because too many things He has told me have come to pass. We can't judge this season by our history with God. I tell my congregation, when you walk or come onto the campus, you are now in my history with God, not yours. It's as if you come into the home of some person and you conduct yourself a little differently because you are not in your house. Please note: there's nothing wrong with benefiting from someone else's sacrifice because that is what most of us are doing and have done anyway. Hear me: this is what we are doing right now! The Bible provides demonstrations of those benefiting from others' sacrifices and today, history speaks that we are benefiting from other's sacrifices. Today, we reap the benefits from Dr. King's sacrifice; we're benefiting from Jesus' sacrifice (the ultimate price, death). Therefore, whatever we are experiencing is not so bad at all compared to those who came before us.

Imagine if you could have been on the whipping post, being beaten with 39 lashes across your back and then nailed to the cross. This has not happened to any of us, so you are in a good place—you are in a God place. I want you to meditate on this and really get it in your spirit; this place is the "new" normal for your life. Scripture provides the context for which we are to follow and to support your life of unprecedented peace, favor and abundance.

Now therefore, in the sight of all Israel, the assembly of the Lord, and in the hearing of our God, be careful to seek out all the commandments of the Lord your God, that you may possess this good land, and leave it as an inheritance for your children after you forever. "As for you, my son Solomon, know the God of your father, and serve Him with a loyal heart and with a willing mind; for the Lord searches all hearts and understands all the intent of the thoughts. If you seek Him, He will be found by you; but if you forsake Him, He will cast you off forever. Consider now, for the Lord has chosen you

*to build a house for the sanctuary; be strong, and do it."
(1 Chronicles 28:8–10, New King James Version)*

On that night God appeared to Solomon, and said to him, "Ask! What shall I give you?" And Solomon said to God: "You have shown great mercy to David my father, and have made me king in his place. Now, O Lord God, let Your promise to David my father be established, for You have made me king over a people like the dust of the earth in multitude. Now give me wisdom and knowledge, that I may go out and come in before this people; for who can judge this great people of Yours?" Then God said to Solomon: "Because this was in your heart, and you have not asked riches or wealth or honor or the life of your enemies, nor have you asked long life— but have asked wisdom and knowledge for yourself, that you may judge My people over whom I have made you king— wisdom and knowledge are granted to you; and I will give you riches and wealth and honor, such as none of the kings have had who were before you, nor shall any after you have the like." So Solomon came to Jerusalem from the high place that was at Gibeon, from before the tabernacle of meeting, and reigned over Israel. And Solomon gathered chariots and horsemen; he had one thousand four hundred chariots and twelve thousand horsemen, whom he stationed in the chariot cities and with the king in Jerusalem. Also the king made silver and gold as common in Jerusalem as stones, and he made cedars as abundant as the sycamores which are in the lowland. (2 Chronicles 1:7–15, New King James Version)

DON'T CHANGE YOUR WORSHIP

Looking closely at the selected scriptures of 1 and 2 Chronicles. The blessings are declared and we find Solomon praying based on the sacrifices of his father David. Solomon receives instruction from the beginning: be faithful to God, don't change your worship. Your father, who wasn't perfect, worshipped Me (God). This is why he repented for the things he had done. Don't turn from your worship. Well, Solomon turned from his worship and we see that Solomon's end was not what it could have been. He had 700 wives and began to worship what his wives, who were from a foreign land, worshipped. God didn't have a problem with the number of wives he had since this practice was acceptable during the biblical time period Solomon lived in; God had a problem with the worship.

One must be careful, because sometimes your turn from worship happens so subtly you don't realize a change has occurred. One indicator that you are turning away from worship is the prioritization of things over God. When you start doing that, you have turned from pure worship. God said, "Have no other god before Me." When He says this, He means don't prioritize anything above Me because, if you do, you're going to end up in the condition of Solomon.

Furthermore, I have learned that whatever you have when you start worshiping, whatever you have achieved through worshiping Him, if you change your worship, He's going to take it from you. The Lord is a cheerful giver, so whatever He gives me, like the ministry, homes and different things I've been blessed with, if I change my worship, if you change your worship, He's coming back to get those gifts and He's going to give them to someone else.

On Christian television, they showed the story of Solomon and the twelve tribes of Israel. God took ten and left Solomon's son with two and the son couldn't govern those two adequately. So, God will come back and retrieve what rightfully belongs to Him when you change your worship.

SPIRITUAL LEADERSHIP

Notice in the scripture text that Solomon didn't ask for riches, wealth, honor, the lives of his enemies or even long life; he asked, "Give me wisdom and knowledge on how to deal with all these people you have entrusted me to lead." It is important that you have a biblical foundation for spiritual leadership. First, a pastor or spiritual leader is not after things for themselves. If you ever meet up with a leader or minister who wants theirs first, they were not sent by the God we serve. They could not have come from God because real people, who are called by God, care about other people and they prioritize others before themselves. So it's not about me getting my car if you don't have a car. This is the nature of the house I shepherd because it is my nature and in my DNA. Spiritual leaders who serve in a ministry are to have the DNA of the father. I firmly understand that the day I become selfish is the day we lose it all. The day you become selfish is the day you risk losing it all. Selfish people are struggling to hold on to what they have because they have changed their worship.

I am not referencing mishaps in life. Things happen, but I am talking about those who are called to lead multitudes of people. Understand, you who are reading, you are a part of a holy and royal multitude of people, you are a great assembly, you are not two or three people, ten or twenty people gathering together a couple of days a week in a building. With this authority, you must ask—what would happen if I erred? Leaders in a church can run off two or three people, but a true God-appointed leader could hurt many more if they don't stay focused on God. As a result, it is important for leaders to know, this isn't your house—this is the house you serve in. You cannot come in with your heart, because nine times out of ten, your heart is not clean. That's why we see the attitude when you didn't get a chance to do what you wanted to do.

Solomon is not asking, "Can I have it my way?" Solomon says, "I am not equipped to deal with the issues of these people I am encountering." He's willing to say, "I am immature; I'm not ready for this assignment." Anyone who jumps up and says that he or she is ready is not called; he or she couldn't be called. A person who is truly called would have the same attitude and posture of Solomon. Understand something: the things he didn't ask for, he received because his priorities were right. Matthew 6:33 has us to "seek first the kingdom of God and His righteousness, and all these things shall be added to you." When you don't prioritize correctly, you won't have "all these things." So Solomon said, "Teach me how to deal with the issues that I'm going to encounter," and many of you reading are saying, "Teach me, show me, give me wisdom and knowledge of how to deal with the issues that are going on."

I can respectfully and honestly write that not everyone wants to know how to deal with your issues effectively, but a real leader wants to know when you have a problem and desires to help bring resolve to it. How do real leaders deal with unruly people who are around disciplined people? How do they keep wolves in the midst from destroying the entire church? Real leaders have to ask God for wisdom. Solomon asked for wisdom.

People are going to come with issues, and the Bible gives us several illustrations, for example, the issues of two harlots. They both became pregnant and had their children at the same time. One, in the middle of the night, rolled over and killed her child, noticed her child was dead, took her dead child, put it over in the other bed with the other woman and took her living child. Then they stand before Solomon and he has to have wisdom as to how to deal with the situation before him. So this is what Solomon does (read your Bible and you will see): he says, "Okay, let's just take out a sword and divide the child and give each of you a half of the child." One woman said, "Okay, that's fine," while the other cried out, "Give the baby to her." Wisdom told Solomon that the one who cares the most must be the child's mother.

Take heed: if you are running around with some folks who don't care, they aren't going to help you. It's the ones that care the most. Everyone who has asked me to pray for them, I don't forget about it. If you ask someone to pray for you, and he or she walks away and forgets about it, or maybe tells you "Aw girl, I forgot," he or she just doesn't care like they should. You must get this, because a lot of people are being misled by people who don't care. There are a lot of people who want to get rich at your expense. It is best to have systems in place that do not allow individuals to be taken advantage of. I will not let anything or anyone take advantage of what God has entrusted to me.

RECEIVING YOUR INHERITANCE

I would not think to talk about Solomon and his legacy without talking about finding and staying connected to your spiritual father. My spiritual father, Apostle Eddie L. Long, and I talk often and, even when he has made several requests from me, I am always quick to respond and open to anything he wants me to do. I don't have that kind of attitude that says I won't answer the phone when my spiritual daddy calls me. It is not advantageous to roll like that. The day I start thinking like that is the day I start thinking that I'm the source. Whenever you become the source over your father, you have just lost everything. You have lost your inheritance.

Now, here it is: Solomon is being told to leave an inheritance to his children and those who are coming after them forever. Is it plausible to receive an inheritance after you have shifted your worship from God and dishonored the spiritual father God has given you? Now, if you believe in your resources and he (your spiritual father) has greater resources than you have, how are you going to think, "I am the daddy"? Stay with me, because if we don't fix this, we cancel out inheritance. It doesn't make sense to get an attitude, and you need the father more than the father needs you. After all, God is the creator and He ordains the father-son relationship in the earth. God orders your steps to bring you into a relationship with your spiritual father for you to be in line for a spiritual inheritance.

Real, called people of God, this is what we are looking for. Again, it does not benefit you or anyone else to follow a phony. God is establishing a generation that wants the real thing. With the guidance of the Holy Spirit, if you are searching for a sound spiritual leader, these four points will help you to identify your called set man or woman of God:

1. He or she never goes for riches, wealth and honor first, ever.

2. He or she seeks the scriptures for truth.

You will not find truth watching Dr. Phil, you are not going to find truth watching Oprah and you surely will not find truth watching Jerry Springer. If you are looking for truth, I encourage you to go to your Bible. You have to have a heart that desires truth when you are reading your Bible. If you read with the wrong heart, you will read something that doesn't exist. You will use the Bible to justify some act you want to do against the will of God. So, as you read your Bible or when you hear a person you believe is preaching truth, you have to really hear. If you are not hearing, you can conjure up in your own thinking a lie that gives you the right to, for example, divorce, or gives you the right to fornicate, or the right to someone else's spouse. You can find enough to justify that two of the same sex can sleep together. You can come up with something. I don't know how, when you are studying your Bible with the right heart, you could think it says that you don't need a pastor. "Have no confidence in men." "Have no confidence in the flesh" and you aren't anything but flesh—that's exactly what's wrong. You can't put your confidence in your fleshly ideas and thoughts. Your flesh has to be nailed to the cross and die. Dead people don't have negative attitudes. You have not died to self nor have you taken up your cross when you have a bad attitude and bad actions that you justify.

3. He or she will be faithful.

You should follow a leader who knows the faithfulness of God and will be faithful in his or her own home, ministry and personal life. He or she will model faithfulness in what they do. You will never know the faithfulness of God if you are spending time under an unfaithful leader. You will never know the faithfulness of God if all you interact with is unfaithful leaders. You must desire faithfulness. There are people you see operating in ways that are disconnected from the character of our Lord and you are still faithful to them. As a result, you will never be faithful. Put some distance between you and them because whatever is on them is contagious! Any person, male or female, who is not faithful to God will not be faithful to you. You can fool yourself if you would like; however, it is best to be real and honest with yourself. Any person who is not faithful to God does not have the ability to be faithful to you. I don't care how much you invest in the friendship, they are not going to be faithful to you; it's not possible. You learn faithfulness from interacting with God. So, I'm looking at an individual who says, "Well I am faithful to God," and I am thinking, "You can't even get to church on time; how are you going to be faithful to God?" It is not deep; if you can't carry out a single task with other people whom you are in relationship with, how are you going to carry out this contract you are in with God? However you are with people in authority over you is how you are with God. However you treat your boss, however you treat your pastor speaks to your attitude toward God. Women—however you treat your husband will indicate how you will act toward God. If you will mouth off at your husband, you will mouth off at God too.

4. He or she will serve God with a willing heart and a loyal mind.

Any person who is not loyal to God will not be loyal to you. We are to serve God with a loyal heart—the Bible doesn't say anything about being perfect; it says with a loyal heart. Not everyone in leadership is loyal. Moreover, we must possess a willing mind. You can't trust people who fight you in their mind. Isaiah 1:19 reminds us that if we are willing and obedient, we shall eat the good of the land. Jesus heard people's thoughts. Real God-called leaders hear people's thoughts. If there is no willingness attached to your actions, then you are not submitted. For example, a person is getting blessed to get the job done but being cursed for their thoughts. I heard this story about a lady who was praying one day. She didn't have any food and she had children; she was praying God would send someone by to give her some groceries. The neighbor next door noticed that this family did not have any food and the neighbor didn't believe in God. The neighbor felt bad, went out and purchased groceries, came and sat them on the porch for her and then knocked on the door. She came to the door, saw the groceries, called the kids and they were all excited about them. The man said, "I told you your God wasn't real. He didn't send any groceries, I bought these groceries." She said, "No, no, no, no, I prayed for groceries and here they are. God is real. He used you to buy me some groceries. God is real." Oh yes He is! I agree with the lady in this story that God will provide for you, no matter whom He has to use to do it. God has assigned me to do a work in the region I am in, and I don't care if the devil has to finance this vision, I'm still going to get it done. As Christians, we don't have to worry about anything. God will hide some stuff from the ignorant and then they'll still be a blessing. That's why it is important to be around solid Christians and to place distance between you and folks who are not speaking kingdom language. Kingdom speakers can make one statement that will transform your life. This is key when you are dealing with God's people and you are asking for wisdom and knowledge.

CHAPTER 3

Peace and Quietness

THE WARRING HAS ENDED

WE ARE IN A SEASON of peace and quietness. As mentioned before, God said this will be an unprecedented, meaning never before experienced, season of peace and quietness. Peace and quietness doesn't mean we don't work. Peace and quietness doesn't mean we don't praise and worship and we don't open our mouths and glorify God. That's not what it means at all. Peace and quietness means there is no chaos among us.

There has been too much noise in the Body of Christ. There's been too much noise in the church. When I talk about noise, I'm not talking about the volume—I'm talking about the chatter; I'm talking about the chaos; I'm talking about the warring. There's been a lot of warring in the house of God. A lot of the warring in the church is a result of the warring within individuals who make up the church. If you are at war within yourself, you will create and engage in war within the church. However, when we enter into a season of peace and quietness, we don't have to worry about the pulpit and we don't have to worry about the pews. When you get peace and quietness, you are no longer tormented by the enemy in you or anyone else. In other words, the warring ends!

PEACE AND QUIETNESS IS FOR BUILDING

David was a man who was acquainted with warring, chaos and confusion, similar to what takes place in a lot of the churches today. Although he was a "man after God's own heart" and desired to build a temple for God, God restrained him from doing so. However, He did charge David with gathering everything that would be required because he was going to use his son, Solomon, to do this great work.

> *Then he called for his son Solomon, and charged him to build a house for the Lord God of Israel. And David said to Solomon: "My son, as for me, it was in my mind to build a house to the name of the Lord my God; but the word of the Lord came to me, saying, 'You have shed much blood and have made great wars; you shall not build a house for My name, because you have shed much blood on the earth in My sight. Behold, a son shall be born to you, who shall be a man of rest; and I will give him rest from all his enemies all around. His name shall be Solomon, for I will give peace and quietness to Israel in his days. (1 Chronicles 22:6–9, New King James Version)*

Solomon was able to enter into a time of peace after the constant chaos of war under David's rule because God was moving him into a season where He wanted to accomplish some things. The first thing we must understand about a season of peace and quietness is that it is designed for building. There was no way for Solomon to build what God wanted him to build as long as war was going on. There was no way he could build the temple the way the Lord wanted the temple built and put things in place the way the Lord wanted them put in place as long as there was war.

Not only did he have the assignment of building the temple, he also had to find the workers who were assigned to help in the building process. Each of the twelve tribes of Israel had a generational assignment from God. So as Solomon began to set the order for the building of God's temple, he had to find the tribes with specific responsibilities and put them in their proper place. He had to find all the singers, the musicians, the priests; he had to go find all these people who were instructed to serve concerning the temple and the church of God. It took time and focus, and you can't focus on a major project like that while you are warring with other people. Just like Solomon, leaders today have to make sure they are recruiting the right people and putting them in the right places because it's a time of peace, a time to build. As God's people, if you are called to serve within a particular ministry, then make sure you are availing yourself, your gifts, your talents to assist your leader in building.

One morning as I was parking my car in front of the church, I saw one of our leaders walking toward the front entrance. He was dressed very nicely, and I rolled down my window and said, "You look like you are going to preach today." His countenance was already preaching as he walked toward the building. See, this particular man I have had to discipline before, but I didn't realize at that time that his struggle was because he was out of place. I don't think he realized it either, so he was creating chaos in the area that he was working in. Now he's one of the happiest males in my church because I got him in his proper place within the ministry. He has been a member of the church for several years, and I have never seen him smile like he smiles now. So when you see him walking, you see peace, you see prosperity, you see joy; all that is in his strut. It radiates from him because he is now in his proper place and very, very productive. Not only does he have peace, but now that area of ministry has peace. I don't have to worry about that area because he's got it covered. Anytime a person gets peace and quietness and is in his or her proper place, he or she is going to get things done, things other people can't get done because other people always have to start over again. They are constantly in a state of "Oops, I messed up! Now I've got to go back and start over again." When you have peace and quietness, you can hear from God before you detour that greatly and you can get back on track or stay on track so that you don't hinder the work of the ministry.

PEACE WITH NO DISTRACTIONS

During this season of peace and quietness, there will not be distractions. This season will produce an atmosphere of calm and ease within the Body of Christ. Why? Because God's people will not be in a war. Everything that God wants done in this season will now flow, and it's not a struggle, not a push, not a shove. As peace and quietness is coming to the spirits of God's people, they are now seeing how they can help to fulfill the vision and the purpose of the house. They begin to focus. When the distractions of warring end, healing is easy, breakthrough is easy, manifestation is easy. Some of you came out of ministries and churches where there was constant distraction caused by warring. You weren't warring with the devil, you were warring with the people—people in leadership and people in the seats! That time is over! In the scripture text, we see that at this particular time in Solomon's life, he's not threatened by war. His enemies are now quiet because he has to focus on the blueprint that God gave him to erect what God told him to erect. Just like Solomon, your haters can't hate you, [insert your name]; the serpents can't bite you, Paul; the lions are not hungry for you, Daniel and the fire can't burn you, Shadrach, Meshach and Abednego. Everything that could oppose and stop you previously can't stop you now, just like it didn't stop the people in the previous examples. In this season, you are now unstoppable! Your issues may have caused distractions in the past but not in this season. Your shame about mistakes you made may have caused distractions in the past but not in this season. Whatever the enemy tried to use to distract you from getting to this place of peace and quietness didn't work because your season is here and it's unprecedented.

PEACE BRINGS MAXIMUM EFFORT

When there is no peace, there is a lack of unity and harmony. People are unable to maximize their efforts to accomplish the purposes of God because they can't work together. In this season, your efforts will be maximized because of the peace that is resting on the Body of Christ. You'll be able to do in one day what others took two or three years to do. Years ago, the church I pastor was small but growing fast and we were in a building that had seating for a maximum of maybe 300 people. One day I was walking around the sanctuary praying, as I still do today, when the Lord said, "I'll do with you in two years what it took other men twenty years to do." I said, "What you say?" but I received what God had prophesied would happen with the ministry. All of a sudden, things started turning, and, in two years, I went to the level where people who had been in ministry for twenty years already were. The growth was phenomenal. So I can tell you right now that God is creating such unity and harmony that what used to take a long time will happen in an instant, in a moment, immediately because of the harmony. You walk in a hospital and empty it out when you've got harmony. You walk in the room where cancer is and cancer has to be evicted because you have harmony. In that day that Solomon was building, there was so much harmony that they were getting things done that others could not do and they were happy. Happiness will be a by-product of the harmony among God's people. They were all in harmony, they were all in agreement, they were all echoing the same message, they were all working toward the same vision, and God was meeting all their needs and mighty things were happening. If God can just get everybody on the same page, there is no telling what we will be able to accomplish. This season, we will maximize our efforts and see God's plan, individually and corporately, come to pass.

PEACE BRINGS PROGRESS

No type of opposition will be able to stop the progress in this season. If you are building inside, the rain outside can't stop you. All storms are exterior in this season. Let me say that again, all storms are exterior in this season. The only way it's going to rain and storm may be in your mind, but all storms that represent opposition from the devil are exterior in this season. Don't get depressed about what you see out of the window; just know that there is a divider between you and it. Just because you can see the storm doesn't mean you are in it. Some of you identify yourself with your surroundings. I govern my surroundings just as Jesus did. Jesus walked on the water. Peter got on the water and became the situation. Jesus then spoke to the situation and a great calm came to the waters. As long as you think it's a part of you, you'll never speak to it. It's hard to get a man or a woman to address themselves as long as he or she feels that the dilemma is a part of him or her. But when you push your dilemma a little further back, then you step over here and point your finger at it and say, "Peace be still"—it has to obey in this season. You can't speak peace to the exterior if you don't have peace in your interior. So now you see why God is giving you a season of peace so that you can speak to your storms and make progress in advancing His kingdom. For some of us, our health has a storm that needs to be spoken to; for some of us, our finances have a storm that needs to be spoken to.

Let me say something right here. I know we have some problems, and most of us are trying to go get our blessing, but we need to bless what we need to bless first and then go get our blessing. If you haven't sowed a seed, there is no need to run out to the field for a harvest. I don't know any farmers who don't sow and then run to the field looking for a harvest every day. You've got to put something in that field to have some expectation for that harvest; so if you didn't put anything in, don't expect a return. That's self-explanatory. The farmer's got good sense. If I didn't invest anything, I don't have a picture of what I invested; then why would I expect a harvest with what I did not invest? Enough said.

The progress that God is setting in place right now requires us to have freedom from our storms, inside and outside. Frame how your season should look and don't allow the situations to dictate to you when you have the power to speak, no, *command* peace to any situation.

PEACE IN YOUR MIND

During this season of peace, your mind will be at rest concerning the work of God. First, answer this question: Am I doing my own work or am I doing God's work? Let me advise you to make sure you are doing God's work because if you do God's work, your thing will work. Too many saints are working hard on things that will produce on their own if you do God's work first. There's some stuff that happens for me so easily and I'm like, "God, what you say!" You can have rest, or peace, concerning laboring for God's house during this season. You have to understand, everybody's not trying to build their own kingdom. Everybody doesn't have their own agenda when it comes to the house of God. Some of us are building God's house and not our own. Some of us are doing God's work and not our own because God is responsible for His house and His work. You build yours, watch yourself struggle. You build His, and watch God bless it. So if your leader's mind and heart are to build God's house and you get involved, you'll get opportunities and it won't stop at one, you'll get one after the other. Some saints in the Body of Christ battle in their minds about God's house because they connected with some leader they should have never been connected to and they got misused. If you are in a good house where the leader operates in integrity, this should bring a certain amount of peace to your mind. Don't let the scars of the past continue to torment you during a season when God wants to bring rest to your mind.

There is a pastor in Birmingham who started a vision to build an edifice from the ground up. He said that when he first started to build, most of his people were struggling. They were on governmental help, but by the time he finished with that building, they were entrepreneurs and they were doing very well. I repeat, he said *by the time they finished building*. What happened? He got them involved with the vision. He got them involved with an assignment from Heaven and God doesn't ever send you out without a paycheck. And it's never fair how God pays you! When your mind is not at war, you can make an investment in God's work. When you get involved with the purpose of God and the plan of God, you receive the resources, the energy, the wisdom and the finances of God.

Sometimes we can become so "churched" that we don't recognize when we have a leader who's not building his or her own kingdom, but is building the kingdom of God. In this season, you have to get over that trouble in your mind, get over that church hurt and get into the kingdom of God because we are in a brand new season. It's time for you to get up off that place of "do nothing," "commit to nothing," "give to nothing" and "sow to nothing" and get in a place where God wants to do something amazing with your life. Whether we like it or not, the season has changed, and, let me help you, there ain't nothing you can do about it! When you enter into the season of the Lord, I don't care what the opposition has been, it can't stop the season. The more opposition tries to stop it, the more it creates a higher wave of it. Because you can't go over it, you have to go under it; so you raise it up and something's moving higher because something's moving under it. It just lifted you to another dimension. There's a movement you don't want to miss in this season of your life, and it's not just limited to where you are. You better get yourself ready because God is doing amazing things. The Lord spoke to me during a worship service recently and said, "It is my time. I have ordained this season for the Body of Christ. I shall manifest my glory."

A PEACEFUL SEASON

And when the queen of Sheba had seen all the wisdom of Solomon, the house that he had built, the food on his table, the seating of his servants, the service of his waiters and their apparel, his cupbearers, and his entryway by which he went up to the house of the Lord, there was no more spirit in her. Then she said to the king: "It was a true report which I heard in my own land about your words and your wisdom. However I did not believe the words until I came and saw with my own eyes; and indeed the half was not told me. Your wisdom and prosperity exceed the fame of which I heard. Happy are your men and happy are these your servants, who stand continually before you and hear your wisdom! (1 Kings 10:4–9, New King James Version)

In the scripture text, the Queen of Sheba has come to visit Solomon because she had heard about the wealth and prosperity of his kingdom. After touring the kingdom and seeing how the people were living such a high quality of life, in verse 8 she states, "Happy are your men and happy are these your servants ..." God's peace is easily recognizable by the results it produces. Even if people can't identify why they feel at ease in a certain environment or around certain people, it is often the result of God- created peace and quietness. This season, that peace and quietness is yours. Maximize your efforts! Speak to your storms! Rest in your mind! Make progress! Build for the kingdom!

PEACE AND QUIETNESS PART 2

Then he called for his son Solomon, and charged him to build a house for the Lord God of Israel. And David said to Solomon: "My son, as for me, it was in my mind to build a house to the name of the Lord my God; but the word of the Lord came to me, saying, 'You have shed much blood and have made great wars; you shall not build a house for My name, because you have shed much blood on the earth in My sight. Behold, a son shall be born to you, who shall be a man of rest; and I will give him rest from all his enemies all around. His name shall be Solomon, for I will give peace and quietness to Israel in his days. (1 Chronicles 22:6–9, New King James Version)

The work of righteousness will be peace, And the effect of righteousness, quietness and assurance forever. (Isaiah 32:17, New King James Version)

As we have previously discussed, in the scripture text (1 Chronicles 22: 6–9), the Lord has spoken to David and David is now speaking concerning Solomon. David is confirming in Solomon what his assignment is and how God was bringing Solomon into a season of peace and quietness to accomplish this purpose. Just as it was in Solomon's day, today, not only is God bringing you into a season of peace and quietness, He's also bringing the people you have the jurisdiction over into a time of peace and quietness. Again, peace and quietness doesn't mean that we're a quiet church, but that we have a quiet spirit; we have a peaceful spirit and that's very attractive to people who have gone through a lot of chaos. Let me announce to the church that the chaos outside has infiltrated inside. So people are looking for people who bring peace. Some of the people I do business with are amazed at how peaceful it feels when they are doing business with me. They don't have to wonder if I'm trying to get over. They don't have to wonder if I've got some other motive because I'm at peace and that peace manifests itself when I'm conducting business and in every area of my life.

RIGHTEOUS WORKS PRODUCE PEACE

Out of the scripture texts, we see that God is really creating an atmosphere conducive to what He wants to do in this time and this season. In 1 Chronicles 22:9 and Isaiah 32:17, we find that doing righteous works leads to peace. Righteous works cannot lead to chaos. You may come into contact with a lot of chaotic people while you are on your way, but if you don't let your peace flee from you when you are dealing with chaotic people, then after a while the peace in you and the peace outside of you are going to match. Every righteous work will produce peace despite the challenges you might face from people or circumstances; the scriptures confirm that righteousness is going to lead to peace. If you're doing righteousness, your destination, according to Isaiah 32:7, is peace. Let me repeat that—the destination of a righteous work is peace.

THE PRODUCT OF PEACE IS QUIETNESS

Besides peace, another effect of righteousness is the assurance of quietness. If you are doing something out of a righteous and pure heart, you are going to wind up in peace. As you continue that work with peace inside of you, it will then bring you into quietness. Quietness doesn't mean you shut your mouth; quietness means confidence. Have you ever seen someone, who was, despite all hell breaking loose, still sitting there as if everything was all right? They have a quietness, they have a peace, and they have a confidence on the inside of them.

Recently, at a funeral I encountered a young lady I had known several years ago. This particular young lady had experienced a very difficult situation that helped me realize how important that confidence produced by peace is to a believer. While this young lady was pulling into a parking space at her school one day, she wasn't sure if she was parking correctly or not. So, she opened the door and leaned out of the car to pull into the space properly. Her foot hit the accelerator, she fell out of the car and the car ran over her. What makes this incident even more upsetting is that she was pregnant at the time.

I was at home this particular morning, sweeping and cleaning out my basement when the call came in about the incident. As my wife told me what happened, my heart went out toward the young lady and the situation because I have a heart for people, especially when they are under attack in the area of health. I am standing there listening and the report is bad—the doctors couldn't stop the bleeding and the child was in jeopardy—but I never stopped sweeping. I told the Lord, "Lord, if you will keep this young lady and her child, I'll continue to set a level of order that I know you want in the church." See, I didn't change my posture because I knew if I did my part of continuing the righteous work in the church, God was going to do His part as God. Within ten minutes, my wife came back and told me that all of a sudden, the bleeding had stopped; the woman and child were going to be fine. The doctors had just said the woman and her child were going to die, but because somebody kept peace, somebody kept quietness, somebody just kept on doing what they knew they were supposed to do, God was able to get in operation.

I'm telling you: in this season, don't operate like others do. God is trying to get us to this place where we are not shaken so easily. Don't let anything ruffle you in this season of your life, because if you operate in the peace and quietness that is resting on God's people, that is resting on the church, you will see a miraculous move of God for you and others connected to you.

PEACE PRODUCES ORDER, WHOLENESS AND WELL-BEING IN THE COMMUNITY

So peace produces quietness and rest, but to truly get the full picture of how important peace is, we have to add one more aspect to our understanding of peace. Peace is "a state of mind, a state of security or order within a community provided by law or custom." Based on the biblical commentaries, peace is a state or order in a community. A community is a group of people who have something in common provided for by law or custom. A church should always be a community; therefore, we should have certain laws or customs that brings forth peace and order. You can never have peace without order. If you think you're going to have peace and everybody is doing whatever they want to do, you are sadly mistaken. There will never be peace in the church, there will never be peace in your home, there will never be peace anywhere if everybody is doing their own thing and voicing their opinion about everything instead of using the Word of God to decide what the order should be. There has to be order to have peace; you can't have peace where there is no order. Wherever there is chaos, there is a breach of peace. So God is saying to David to tell Solomon, "I'm going to bring peace. I'm going to bring some order in your season."

Peace in Hebrew is the word *shalom*. Where shalom is, God is. When God joins you to a vision, a purpose or an assignment, you should bring peace to that vision, purpose or assignment by following the order established by its leader; within the church, this refers to the set man or woman of the house, the pastor. The order produced

46

by peace within a church ministry means the righteous ways, structure or instructions of God that are in place to bring that vision to pass. Because you are not an enemy or opponent, because you're not trying to change the righteous way a ministry is doing things, the peace (shalom) in you should bring order within that church body, to your pastor as well as your brothers and sisters in Christ. Using the greeting "shalom" means you are saying, "I'm not trying to change what you're doing—I'm just trying to find my place in what you are doing."

I was in a conversation with this couple I met. They were extremely gifted and were in a time of transition and uncertainty about where they should serve within the church. They were talking about the order or the structure of how a certain church, where they had been members, was operating. I listened for a moment, and then I said, "The problem is not them (the church); they've been doing that for years. The problem is you. God has changed what He is doing in you and you want them to come into compliance with it." I wouldn't allow them to go any further talking about change that was only taking place with them and blaming the church. It was not the church. That church had had that structure for years and was successful at what they were doing because they weren't struggling financially or in any other way. The problem was God was doing something different in that couple. Listen to me carefully: when God starts doing something different in you, don't create chaos in the environment you are in. Don't try to change the order because you changed. Amen! Somebody got delivered right there.

Shalom also means wholeness and well-being. So the end result of all that we do is to see people made well. We want people to be whole because peace has to do with wholeness. Shalom equals wholeness, which is produced by order. The only way you can bring anyone or anything into wholeness is by bringing that person or that situation into the order that was designed for them or it by God. It's not just a greeting, yet most people have turned it into a casual greeting. When you meet some people, they say, "Shalom." The question is, "Are you really wanting me to be whole?" When you say shalom to me, you are saying, "I wish that you were whole, I wish that you would remain whole." If you are saying "shalom" and you don't want me to be whole, complete, and in order, you don't want my health to be in order, you don't want my finances to be in order, you don't want my relationships to be in order, then you are using shalom incorrectly.

THE OPPOSITE OF PEACE

God promised Solomon that He would bring peace and quietness. I want to tell you the negative side of what most of us experience in church, the opposite of peace. In this particular season that they had come into in 1 Chronicles 22: 6–9 , there had to be a decrease in war; there had to be a decrease in quarreling; there had to be a decrease in enmity, which is mutual hate; there had to be a decrease in hostile feelings toward others. You can never have peace when there is warring, when there is quarreling, when there is enmity and when you have hostile feelings toward your brothers and sisters; you can never have peace and you can never have quietness. In fact, these are the things that flow from the fruit of unrighteousness. So if you are flowing in righteousness, it's impossible to be at war with your brothers and sisters. That's not a part of righteousness— that's a part of unrighteousness. It's impossible to have hostile feelings toward your brothers and sisters and think you are in righteousness. You are not in righteousness because righteousness is something that Jesus paid for that we didn't deserve. So if you understand that Jesus paid for it, gave it to us and we didn't deserve it, then you can think about people who may have hurt, mistreated or offended you but need you to love them and care about them even if they didn't earn it. If you properly interpret and understand the righteousness you've been given that you didn't deserve, you understand that you've got to extend some of that righteousness toward the person who hurt you, even if it's your husband or wife. When you know how Jesus placed righteousness on you, that's the peaceful part of it. There was nothing you or I could do to earn it. I was messed up. I was beaten up. I was about to quit and Jesus put righteousness on me. I know I didn't measure up, so when my brothers and sisters don't measure up, the same righteousness He put on me, I put on them because they are not perfect but we serve a perfect Savior. You must do the same thing—extend to others the righteousness you have been freely given. If we just trust Him and rely on Him, He'll do the same thing for them as He has done for us. We must get rid of the quarreling, we must get rid of the warring, we must get rid of the hostile feelings and we must get rid of the hatred in the church. I can truly say that I love the people who have tried to hurt me just as much as I love the people who love me and have said only good things about me. Why? Because the ones who hate me and said things about me didn't have a revelation of how much they were going to need me. When you are in trouble, you need somebody to look beyond your faults and see your need. You need somebody in your life who understands that your behavior is a result of your past. While you were in that mode where you couldn't protect yourself, something happened and you need somebody who can see into the depths of your past and then turn around and point to your future and say, "No matter how much you scream and kick, I'm going to help you get to your future." That's what you need in your life. God provides that through a God-sent, anointed man or woman of God (pastors, apostles) who can speak into your life and cause you to move forward into your destiny and purpose. Don't let warring hinder you from what God wants to do for you in this point of time in your life. So the quietness has to come, and the warring has to cease because of the accomplishment God wants to occur in this season.

PEACE TO MOVE INTO DESTINY

Quietness means to rest. Quietness also means confidence. In that basement that day while I was sweeping, I had to stay in peace and quietness. We quote, "I shall not be moved," but do we live it? You must be settled; you must be confident in the God you serve, who can do anything but fail. I want to encourage you to remain in that peace and quietness, no matter what. It doesn't matter what comes my way. I'm quiet in my spirit now. It can't change anything. I'm not going to let anybody remove the order because the order is what keeps it quiet. The devil is so afraid that there will be quietness on the inside of you because if you ever get quiet, you're going to hear from God. If you ever get quiet, you're going to build something that man cannot build. If you ever get quiet, you're going to do something that generations before you were never able to do. It's been so noisy on the inside of us for so long, if it gets quiet, we get scared. We say quotes like "there's quiet before the storm." I want to tell you that the storm is over; now it's quiet time. God is bringing some peace and quietness in your spirit and whatever He's been trying to say to you for the last ten years, you're going to hear it this year. Everything that deterred you from where God wanted to take you, you're about to hear it down in your spirit. There's about to be a settling, whether you're a male or female, black, white,

Hispanic, Asian, because God is bringing a quietness down on the inside of you. It doesn't matter what your past has been because God is bringing a quietness on the inside of you that assures you that you have a great future and one thing about it, nobody can take my destiny from me. Why? Because I'm quiet, I'm settled and I'm confident in the name of the Lord.

"Cast not away your confidence because it has great recompense of reward." I'm considered arrogant by people who don't know how to have a quiet spirit. I'm just sure that whatever I preach, God's going to bring back a harvest. I'm sure if I do works of righteousness, God's got to give me some peace. If I've done what I'm supposed to do, now God has to do what He said He would do. Let me confirm that God's about to do what He said He would do for you as well. Why? Because you are coming to a place of peace, you're coming to a place of rest, you're coming to a place of quietness in your spirit and the devil has to flee because he doesn't know what to do when you get quiet in your spirit. You're starting to have confidence.

Confidence is contagious. Everybody wants it. A lot of people are doing things, but they have questions about what they are doing. However, when you become confident, when you settle into that quietness, you are about to accelerate into your future. I have a level of confidence, not arrogance, that I'm in my right place at the right time, and that I'm exactly where the Lord wants me to be. You can have that confidence, too, when you let shalom rule in your life.

Colossians 3:15 says, "And let the peace of God rule in your hearts." You will be amazed at what you attract when you get peace and quietness. So many environments have been tormented by chaotic people, but now that you are catching the spirit of the Lord, you bring something into that environment that settles that environment. Just as Jesus spoke over the water and said, "Peace, be still," and it did not rebel against Him, the environment you speak over cannot rebel against you when you have peace and quietness within you. The waters have to settle, the winds have to cease and everything has to calm down. In this season, if you open up, everything has to settle down. Every mouth has to speak blessings and not curses. This is no season for cursing—this is a season of destiny and blessings. Overflow in your life right now. You are moving into the life that God wanted you and generations before you to live. God wants a people to obtain some things to show that He is God.

A PEACEFUL LIFE

I want to make an announcement: God is about to prove to everybody that He is God through your life. There's a peace that surpasses all understanding coming on your life right now. There's a quietness of your mind. You're no longer tormented by the adversary. The devil is in trouble when you start speaking it and it starts manifesting. You may not have the vocabulary to identify or clarify what the Lord is doing right now, but what you've been looking for is here right now. If you want it, it's easy to receive it. Just let yourself go, and the Spirit of the Lord will sweep across your life and every situation in your life and bring peace and rest to you. Let me explain what the warring has been about. Some people say it's over the anointing on your life; I say it's about you surviving for this season. You are now in a day that's not going to cheat you. In this day, even those who try to cheat you will not be successful. I call you to a place of rest because your adversaries are not going to capitalize on you in this season. Even when there is a strategy or attempt, it's still going to work out for your good, according to Romans 8:28, because you love the Lord and you're the called according to His purpose. You're reading this book because you have purpose and you're lining it up with the Lord. The devil warred to keep you out of order and disjointed because if you ever got in your place, Ephesians 4 says, "every joint supplieth." The enemy was afraid you were going to get in your place and get your supply because when you get your supply, every devil in your region and your bloodline is in trouble. Amen, Amen, Amen.

CHAPTER 4

Accommodations from on High

But Jesus said to him, "Put your sword in its place, for all who take the sword will perish by the sword. Or do you think that I cannot now pray to My Father, and He will provide Me with more than twelve legions of angels?" — Matthew 26: 52–53 (New King James Version)

H ERE, JESUS IS SPEAKING TO Peter and He says, "This is not a time for warring Peter. I've got everything at my disposal that I need so just put your sword back up." We can see in the scriptures that the Spirit of God moves before us. As He moves before us, He drives out things that are occupying what belongs to us. These are the things that we should be possessing. What things should you possess?

Out of heaven He let you hear His voice, that He might instruct you; on earth He showed you His great fire, and you heard His words out of the midst of the fire. And because He loved your fathers, therefore He chose their descendants after them; and He brought you out of Egypt with His Presence, with His mighty power, driving out from before you nations greater and mightier than you, to bring you in, to give you their land as an inheritance, as it is this day. (Deuteronomy 4: 36–38, New King James Version)

He will also go before Him in the spirit and power of Elijah, 'to turn the hearts of the fathers to the children,' and the disobedient to the wisdom of the just, to make ready a people prepared for the Lord. (Luke 1: 17, New King James Version) [Note: Jesus is talking about John the Baptist in this passage.]

When God gets ready to do something, there is a force that moves ahead of you to accommodate you. The word accommodate means "to make fit." What God is doing in this particular season (this season of unprecedented peace, favor and abundance) is accommodating and structuring things in order for you to fulfill His purpose, not your purpose. The purpose of a church (outside of God's purpose) can be selfish and self-seeking. Therefore, if a church is allowed to move in its own purpose, the people will turn completely from the will of God. Turning from the will of God correlates to living without Him, and I don't want to know what it's like to turn away from God. I've done too much with Him to live without Him.

God is accommodating you and making things suitable for where you are going. While Jesus was walking the earth, He would send His disciples out to various places. Every place that He sent them was already set and ready to accommodate them before they arrived. For those of you who are sitting where you have been sitting for the last few years and thinking the way you've been thinking, there's nothing to accommodate you where you are right now. You have stalled and stopped short of your accommodations. Your accommodations are ahead of you. The things that fit you are ahead of you. Don't stay where you are physically, mentally and financially. There are no accommodations in your current location, so it's not going to fit. Keep moving forward.

In the scripture text, Peter pulls out his sword and thinks that he can protect Jesus. Jesus said, "No, no, no, I've got twelve legions of angels at my disposal right now. If I called on them, they would show up right now. I don't need you to do something fleshly to try to help me right now. What I need is to go through this because what I'm supposed to do is on the other side of this. So, Peter put your sword up; stop being fleshly; stop doing what you've learned in the world and let's hook up with Heaven because Heaven has a whole lot to offer in this season."

Jesus said that 12 legions of angels were at His disposal right then. In the Roman army, a legion contained 6,000 men. So there were more than 72,000 angels at Jesus' disposal right there on the spot. Jesus doesn't need one man with a sword who doubts sometimes and believes sometimes. He's got more than 72,000 angels. All He has to do is open His mouth and everything and everyone around Him would have to drop their rocks.

So, this force of unseen beings are in operation. I want to tell you that you are not alone. Whenever you start talking about legions, you're talking about rank and flanks. Flanks refer to those who are walking with you, so there are angels you can't see that are walking with you. After a Wednesday night service, a woman said to me, "Bishop, I saw these big old angels on the side of you." She's got to be right, because there's no way you could get me to do what I'm doing without some help. I've got plenty of help on my side.

Again, Jesus said, "I've got more than twelve legions of angels; I've got 72,000 unseen beings helping me right now." Let me tell you how these things work. You want to see angels, but I just want to see results. You say, "Lord, let me see an angel." I say, "Lord, let me see the results of what the angels do." You want to see over into a spiritual realm, but let the physical realm line up with what God said. You don't need to see an angel; you need what was wrong to become right. That's a sign to you that the angels showed up when you started praising. In this season, you can't do low level praise because when you open your mouth, the angels get into motion. When I start preaching, the atmosphere starts shifting. You want to know why? Because an angel goes in every direction once the sound of my voice begins to project into the room. When I open up my mouth, the unseen realm begins to become activated and things begin to work on my behalf. Angelic hosts begin to cover the entire campus as a result of me opening my mouth. They not only go to work when I open my mouth—they go to work when you open yours. When you need to get something done, open your mouth and activate your angels to take action. You are not alone!

HEAVENLY FORCES ARE WORKING ON YOUR BEHALF

There are some things happening for you that you didn't have to touch. Guess what? When you began to read this book, you made up in your mind that you were going to obey; so now your angels are released on your behalf to work miracles, signs and wonders. What you couldn't physically change, they're changing right now. Someone may say, "That's spooky." No, that's God! They may be spooky, but God's real.

There are forces that work on our behalf to facilitate in a region we cannot reach physically. For example: It was going one way and then all of a sudden, the next day it changed. You prayed in your bedroom, and the situation changed across town or in another state. What do you think happened? Some people may say, "It must have been the Lord." No, it wasn't "must have been"— it *was* the Lord. When you open your little mouth and start saying things to God, He releases angels. God's not leaving Heaven, but He's got an army at your disposal. If you would just open your mouth, they would be there to accommodate you.

I believe that everything should go the way that the Word says it should go. There were some things that weren't going the way that I thought they should go. I put the Word in the atmosphere because the Bible says that the Word shall not return void. The angels don't respond to cursing, but they respond to the Word. If you start praising, a breakthrough will happen just like that. Start giving God what He asked you to give Him and watch that army march on your behalf.

In the book of Deuteronomy, He said that He drove those out who were mightier and stronger than us. That means that there was some force ahead of them at work. Let's take a look at some Bible history. In the Bible, Gideon didn't hit anyone; all he did was take some lanterns and torches and hit them together. All of a sudden, the enemies turned on one another. The whole Midianite army was self-slaughtered. When you begin to praise, your enemies will start to turn on one another. They'll wonder why they can't get along. It's because you're releasing something into the atmosphere. When you release something into the atmosphere, God's heavenly hosts go into operation, and the thing that wanted to destroy you is now being destroyed.

Jehoshaphat was being opposed by Mt. Seir and Ammon. They said they were going to take him down. Jehoshaphat said, "Hey you all, come here, let's consult together. We are going to start praising, worshipping and giving God glory." The Bible says that when they got to the other side of the hill, their enemies had slaughtered themselves. It's not about praying anything bad toward someone; it's about praising the Lord.

A NEW BEGINNING

You have to understand what God is doing in these years of unprecedented peace, favor and abundance. He's doing exceedingly, abundantly more than he did in the past. Jesus said "Greater works shall you do because I am going to the Father." If He can do that, then what are you sweating about now? Why do you have anxiety? You don't have anything to worry about in these years. These years are settled in concrete by God! They are already sealed in the heavenlies and they now exist in the earth realm. All things are possible to him or her who believes. All things are working together for the good of those who love the Lord and are called according to His purpose (Romans 8:28). All things are working together for the good because we love God and not only do we love God, but we are called according to His purpose. Everything and every situation is working together for our good. We're becoming the head and not the tail. We're above only and not beneath because all things are working together for our good. It's too late to say what's not going to happen when it's already happening. You can't turn this around. This is a God moment. This is not a moment of stressing, this is a moment of rest and peace, a moment to quiet your mind. This is not a moment to fight against what is advancing you. This is a new beginning.

In order to have a new beginning, you have to have an ending. Something has to end in order for God to give you a new beginning. If you just go ahead and let that old thing die, that new thing will come to the surface. Let it go! In order for you to get where you need to be, you have to give up where you are and go back to where you originally started. Have you had things you really didn't want but you tolerated it? Is pride stopping you from letting go of what is not working? Are you so afraid of how you will look to people that God can't get you to your next destiny? When you know that you've got legions of angels with you, you can let go of what does not work. Readjust yourself because what you have, you obtained through anxiety and restlessness. You may have gotten an Ishmael when an Isaac was on the way. Be careful when you get anxious. You'll get something that won't work for you. Say this aloud, "In a few more days, what I should have had originally, I shall have it. In a few more days, because I am willing to give up what isn't working, I will have what God promised would work." The no's put you where you didn't want to be; now there are nothing but yes's. This is a yes season, but you're stuck in the no's that put you where you didn't want to be. It's time for you to move over into the yes's that push you beyond where you should be. You need to start practicing and stop pausing when you get a yes. You're pausing because you used to have a no. As soon as you get a yes, say, "Amen." Get the paperwork and go on about your business. Stop trying to reason and rationalize in your mind how it worked out in your favor. Just start saying, "Thank you."

Others don't understand what is released ahead of you. They don't understand the rankings that are marching with you. If they did, they wouldn't do what they do. They don't understand that you will survive only because you have enough rankings with you (that they can't see) to keep you going. Your help can't be seen by them because they want you to look to man, but you will look to the hills. When you start saying, "God I'm still going to praise you, I'm still going to worship you and I'm still going to believe you," your help comes.

You're in one of those moments that just doesn't make any sense at all. You have some family members who are going to be looking at you. You are about to silence them because things that are happening for you won't make any sense at all. They are going to grab their computers and begin YouTubing and Googling, trying to figure out how you do what you do. However, they can't Google or YouTube this because it won't make sense. People told me, "Well Mr. Davis, this is what we do." I said, "Thank you, but this is what you're going to do." They did what I told them that they were going to do.

There's this commercial where a girl tells someone that her credit score is a 780 (or something like that); then she kicks her foot up on the table and says, "Now tell me what you are going to do for me? What else are you going to throw into this thing?" You have to have that type of confidence and believe that God is able to do anything but fail. If you've got faith, you need to sit down and say, "Now I'm going to tell you, I'm framing up my future right now with my words and this is what is about to happen according to the Word of God." Then kick your feet up and say, "Now what are you going to do for me?"

BELIEF IN THE WORD IS FAITH

Some preachers just preach because it's their Sunday or Wednesday responsibility. I don't function like that. I go to my church on Wednesday and Sunday because I'm going to tell the congregation what "thus says the Lord" concerning them. When I left home one afternoon, I felt the anointing the closer that I got to the house of the Lord. Now, at that time there were only a few people on staff there, but the closer I got to the house, the more I began to feel the presence of God. I said, "God this is good" so when I went in, I had a level of expectation. I knew that God was up to something and I wasn't trying to figure out how it was going to happen—I just had something leaping in my spirit knowing that "it's already done." I know that you've been talking to too many secular people and people on the job. They try to tell you, "Don't believe that stuff. It doesn't work." It didn't work for them because they didn't believe it. It works for you because you believe it! Belief in the Word is faith. Never take the Word and try to make it work without faith in the Word. When you use the Word, you've got to have faith in it.

The Word is seed, and if you ever get seed into good soil, it will produce for you. You might say, "Well Bishop, I heard what you said last week and I went in there and spoke to my checkbook, and nothing has changed." When you want a financial breakthrough, but you don't have anything but lint in your pockets, you should touch the collection plate (offering bucket), and then go home and speak to your checkbook. You've got to get some substance into the ground to expect a harvest. What do you need for a faith project? You need a man of God for your faith project.

It was my spiritual father's birthday, so I sent him a seed on behalf of the church and on behalf of my family. I said "Okay, I'm going to seal this thing." It's already going well but I want to surf! I just sent him something and I knew it was sealed. I got the report of my seed a few days later. What I was believing for, I got. See, I know how to work that thing. It's not about the man of God trying to get money out of you; it's about you having a faith project. There's no need in believing in something that you're not willing to invest in. My family will never struggle because I sealed the deal. When you seal the deal, there's no devil in hell that can take from you what God has given you. What are you believing for? You can have it. In this season, it's not restricted from you. There are no demons or forces that can stop it. Your worst enemy can't stop this one. You might as well give them a hug because they can't stop you. There are forces with you that are much more than the world against you. There are heavenly hosts that have been dispatched on your behalf. You're wondering why God would think so much of you to send you help. Because you're in His purpose, and when you get into His purpose, He'll send you help. You're going to wonder why these things are happening. Because somewhere in the middle of your trying, you gave up and that's when God reached way down to pick you up.

There are forces that want to keep you down, that want to restrict you from obeying God, but the Bible says that the disobedient are being turned to the just. I understand that you've been hurt, but the only way you can get healed is if God puts a challenge to your obedience in front of you. It's going to hurt all the way to the altar and all while you're carrying out your act of obedience because you've been through something. Although you've been through something, don't let it define who you are.

"So, Bishop are you saying that all the way to my destination it's going to be painful?" Yes, it will be painful, but not physically; it's in your mind. Your mind will try to talk you out of obedience, but still keep walking forward. Your mind may tell you all sorts of things: Don't do it; Don't trust it; They are just after your money; You know how they do in church. But before the devil can get you convinced, something will start to happen on your behalf. You've got help!

EXPECTATION FOR ACCOMMODATIONS

SEEK THE LORD IN THE DESIGNATED SEASON

Do you have great expectations for some things? I'm going to tell you how to get there. I'm going to tell you how not to miss it. It's time for you to move into a new dimension. Hear me now, or your neighbor is going to be in a new dimension, and you are still going to be sitting in an old dimension. This is the most favorable season that your lifetime and your neighbor's lifetime will ever see. It doesn't get any better than this. I am sure that some of us will still be here after Jesus calls the first group home because we didn't believe that Jesus was coming, so we didn't prepare. If we don't prepare, we are going to miss the first ride. We are going to know who the Antichrist is. I don't want to know who he is. I don't want to be here. I'm not going to be here. So if you don't believe that, read your Bible.

Seek the Lord while he may be found, Call upon him while He is near. (Isaiah 55:6, New King James Version)

Isaiah 55:6 tells us that there's going to be a period of time when it's going to be difficult to find Him, but that's not this season. The verse also tells me that if I call upon Him while He is near, there may be a time that He is distant. That lets me know that I need to take advantage of the moment. We know that the sun sits in the sky. In the summertime, our part of the planet is closer to it than we are in the wintertime. Therefore, the temperature changes. It's not that the sun stops shining in the winter, it's just a different season.

Right now, the Body of Christ is closer to the Son, Jesus Christ. It is a critical time in the Body of Christ and we have been living like the world for so long that we aren't making the necessary adjustments. We don't realize what message God's been trying to get to us. Don't do your normal thing. Don't prepare your normal way. Don't go to church thinking the same way and expecting nothing. Have you been expecting nothing for so long and not getting anything? If so, do you wonder why God isn't moving for you? It's because you didn't expect God to do anything for you.

We're now in the season of the Lord. I know you want the glory and I know that you're rat racing, trying to get money and success. If you get God, you get all of that. "Seek ye first the kingdom of God and His righteousness and all these things shall be added unto you" (Matthew 6:33). Do you think that I'm going to run to the job and volunteer to work overtime when I've got time to seek the Lord? I am not working overtime; I'm going to seek some God time. You need God more than you need overtime. All that time spent working overtime should be spent calling on the Lord. If you are working overtime, you are missing His time.

Here it is a time and a season that we should seek. That means that we should go for a search of Him. It's not going to be hard in this season. Have you ever gone to church and wondered how the atmosphere got so filled with the Spirit? It happens when someone creates it. So you don't have to work for it, but you do need to learn how to enjoy it. You can never get a great atmosphere without someone making a great sacrifice. When a great sacrifice is made, an atmosphere is produced where God hangs around. God never hangs around an atmosphere where there is no sacrifice. You can read the Bible from the front to the back cover and see that everywhere there was a sacrifice, God showed up.

He says call on His name while He is near. That means that there is sometimes a distance between us. In your Bible and in my Bible, there is a designated season that God does great things for God's people, not just anybody, but God's people. I know a young man who went to the doctor. They were going to drain a tumor and it had shrunk. The next time they looked, it was gone! This is a prime example of God doing something great for His people in the designated season.

A TIME FOR PURIFICATION AND CLEANSING

Therefore submit to God. Resist the devil and he will flee from you. Draw near to God and He will draw near to you. Cleanse your hands, you sinners; and purify your hearts, you double-minded. (James 4: 7–8, New King James Version)

He's right there. If you make a step forward, He'll make a step forward. If you want Him, He'll want you. In fact, when you don't want Him, He still wants you. The problem is that you've got to cleanse your hands and purify your heart. Anytime you are coming into the season of the Lord, you don't do church as usual. There are seasons that you need to maximize in, and this is one of them.

A lot of people are expecting great things, but they have dirty hands. That thing that you have been dreaming about and confessing will not come to pass unless you cleanse your hands and purify your heart. Every time you come into a holy season or approach a holy season, you should go into a time of consecration. You never walk into that season with a bunch of bitterness, resentment, hatred and selfish ambition. You need to clean your hands from all the stuff you got caught up in. You need to clean your heart form all the idolatrous worship you've been in. Everything that you prioritize ahead of God, you need to start cleaning it up. This season will work better for you than any other season has worked in your life, but you've got to make the effort. God's not going to do it. He said that you're supposed to do it. Most of us are challenged when it comes to hearing the Word and we rebel because we are dirty. We resist when we are not clean. When our hearts are not right, we resist the truth. I can tell when a person's heart is not right because they go into resistance mode.

What have you gotten caught up in that God wants to clean up? What have you gotten tied into where you have forsaken God? He said, "Return to Him." You would not need to return if you hadn't walked away. What has caused you to walk away from God? What has caused you to give up on God? I'm trying to get something to you and get you back to the God you should be worshipping and serving. You may say, "Well, I'm not into all of this church stuff." It has nothing to do with church stuff. If God stopped working, you will stop breathing right now. If there's not a respirator to put you on real quick, you won't be here. It doesn't matter what your age is, because there are teenagers dropping on the basketball court right now because they don't have a respirator of the Holy Ghost.

We've had enough "funky" worship to last us a life-time. Whenever we approach God to worship, we should cleanse our hands and our hearts. Every born again believer doesn't need to be pumped up when it's time to praise God. When your hands are clean and your heart is pure, all of a sudden you hear a song, your hands will shoot up, your mouth comes open and praise starts being released form your mouth because it is from your heart. "From the abundance of the heart," the mouth starts singing. You get credit for ignorance before this moment, but there is no more credit for your ignorance after now. So, it's no longer ignorance but rebellion.

He says, "I'm ready to come near you, but I'm so holy, if I come near you and your hands are dirty and your heart is impure, I'll kill you." The very nature of God is not like the average church person you come into contact with. The nature of God is like light dispelling and destroying darkness. Darkness can no longer exist when the lights are on. That's why most people are at their worst when they are in darkness. Everything straightens up when the lights come on. He says, "There's something that I want to do for you, through you and with this region, but I need you to go and clean your hands. Everything you've been handling that had nothing to do with Me, you need to go cleanse your hands from it."

The heart is desperately wicked. Who can know it? Anybody who does not know the Word can't discern your heart. That's why the church doesn't preach the Word. If they don't preach the Word, there is no discernment of the heart. When you are a Word person, you can look through the eyes of an individual and discern what is going on in their heart. The Word is a discerner of the intent of the heart. Some people may say, "You don't know what I'm up to." Yes, I do if I get a Word that you are up to no good.

IF YOU ARE NOT GIVING, YOU ARE TAKING

Every real saint is looking for an opportunity to give. They are not willing to take until they give. I won't take worship until I give worship. When you are truly born again, you are looking for an opportunity to give. You ask, "How can I help?" not "How can I get paid?" How can I contribute or make life better for others? The true sign that you've been born again is that you look for somebody to help and not somebody to take advantage of. I've given more than I've ever taken from everybody I'm in relationship with. I am the biggest giver at my church. My wife and I are the biggest givers because I'll always give more than I'll ever take. That's why I'm blessed, because blessed is the one who gives. It is more of a blessing to give than to receive.

I don't want to learn how it feels to be waiting on a check from the government. No, I'm going to be furnishing the government with checks. No, I don't always want to be the recipient of governmental help. I want to be the one making an investment in governmental help. It is more blessed to give than to receive, and if you are in that area of needing aid from the government, you're not going to stay there. This season is shifting you right out of governmental support. God's getting ready to load you down where you are now financing different programs and organizations that are going to make things better for another man. He says, "I'm coming closer and if I'm coming closer, what you need to do is cleanse your hands. You don't need to have wrong motives. You need to get your heart right and purify your heart."

PURIFY YOUR HEART

Some people say, "I want a move of God," but how could they with an unclean heart and a rebellious spirit? They don't want God to come. The last time God showed up around rebellion, He kicked it out of Heaven. That's why churches are structured to keep God out. When God comes in, He deals with those who won't prepare for Him. So they keep God out, don't have a pastor who really loves God, keep a pastor who does a little something extra on the side, so the congregants can do a little something extra in their own lives, too. Whenever you get a real pastor, it puts a demand on you to stop gossiping and fighting your brothers and sisters. Instead of gossiping and fighting, the very time I feel something a bit ill toward someone, God makes me sow an offering into them. You need to get some money and give it to the person you are annoyed with, jealous of, or putting down, right now. You should do this because your money and your heart are tied together. If you give them some money, it will release your heart. Anytime I feel this irking on the inside, I start writing out a check, because I'm going to keep my heart free before God. I'm not going to let some little issue that somebody doesn't even know anything about hold me down in a season like this.

You have missed too many seasons already. It's not because they didn't come by. You may have missed some seasons because you had dirty hands and a filthy heart. The devil knows that if he can keep the saints (people of God) with dirty hands and filthy hearts, everything that God wants to release to them, he can block it. Whenever God is moving, I know that I need to do something about my hands. I may have handled something that I should not have handled. Therefore, I make sure that my hands are clean and my heart is pure during a move of God.

When you walk into the house of God with a heavy heart, take it to the altar. Everything that weighs on your heart should be placed on the altar. You can't give God the praise and worship that He deserves with a heavy heart. If you don't take it to the altar, you're not going to be able to receive all that you're supposed to receive. Don't just go to church and plop down and act like, "Bishop better be glad I'm here." Nobody will be glad that you are there because if you don't release it, it is going to block up something.

You have been blocked up long enough. God said, "This is a season that I have an open Heaven, and I'm tired of you walking around holding and harboring all that stuff in your heart and coming before me with dirty hands. I'm ready to release a blessing on this region, but you keep getting in My way." There's no devil that is stopping anything. It's dirty hands and impure hearts that is stopping everything. The devil is not stopping miracles or financial breakthroughs. It's people running around with dirty hands and impure hearts. There's no way that the devil can rule in a season like this. "Blessed are the pure in heart for they shall see God." Manifestation time is right now!

Wash your hands, purify your heart and then shall the King of Glory come in. "Bishop, who is the King of Glory?" you ask. He is the Lord strong and mighty. You don't want to fight me while the Lord's on my side. The Lord is mighty in battle. The battle is not yours. The battle is the Lord's. Shout praises to the God who is fighting your battles. Your praise will become someone's nightmare. Keep praising your God.

CLEANSE YOUR HANDS

You're going to be surprised at what God is going to let you handle when you start cleaning your hands. You're going to be surprised at the amount of money that is going to come through your hands when you clean your hands. God can't put money in your hands until you clean your hands. The only people who will want to stop you are those who have dirty hands and filthy hearts. Those who are clean will know what your motives are, know what you represent and know who hired you.

I understand when you don't trust because you're not trustworthy. My first thought is that everybody is faithful and loyal like I am, so I've been filled with a lot of disappointment over the years. However, I keep washing my heart. When you get a clean heart, you think that everybody's going to do what they say because you do what you say you're going to do. If your first thought is negative, you need to ask God to help you in your heart.

If you are going to lead in such a move of God, you have to make sure that your hands are clean and your heart is pure. You cannot lead a move of God with dirty hands. I can't want another man's wife while I'm trying to do what I do. So I keep my hands in the right place to keep them clean. Clean hands stay with the same woman all their married years. I've stayed in the same bed for 26 years and I'm going to be in the same bed for another 26 years. No wonder you don't trust anybody—you can't trust yourself. I thought that all men loved their wives the way I love my wife. I thought that every man was caught up into their beautiful woman because I'm caught up with mine and I don't need anyone else. She is more than enough for me. I can look at her and see how much God loves me. I don't need a substitute as long as my hands are clean and my heart is pure. A substitute is a prostitute.

When you want to be faithful, get around faithful people. When you want to keep being a pimp, keep running with the guys you're running with. I have to be careful around other people because they may try to imitate everything I do and they go home and reproduce it in their homes. For example, I have a spiritual son who mirrors and echoes me. If I beat my wife, he may go home and beat his wife, but if I love my wife, he's going to go home and love his wife. If I provide for my family, he's going to provide for his family.

BRINGING EVERYTHING INTO ORDER

I just believe that if I can bring you into order with the feasts of the Lord, you can break every generational bondage that has been passed down for one to two hundred years. You can't second-guess yourself when you're in leadership. Get with God and get your hands clean and your heart purified, so that you can tell the people what says the Lord. You can get on this ride and tell people about it after you get off, or you can wonder what the ride was all about. You have people who are tied to you who God wants to free. God wants to do something for them. In order to do something for them, He's got to do something for you.

Never be so isolated and juvenile in your thinking that it's all about you. God would never have allowed you to read this book if He wasn't thinking about you. When your family members (who have never been to church) start going with you, it's not you they are following. It's God who's manifesting in your life that causes them to follow you. It's something that God puts on you; it's a grace and a favor. He will lace your words so that they will have an impact on the hearers you speak to. You have to learn to give God the glory. If He ever takes His hands away, guess what? You are going to go back to all of those insecurities, struggles and traumas. They are still there. God just lifted you up above them. I realize where I came from, so I keep my hands clean and my heart pure because I don't ever want to go back to that place. I want to keep living my dream because I got tired of living my nightmare. If you are fed up with a nightmare, cleanse your hands.

Jesus washed His disciples' feet. Then He said, "The preaching of the Word is like the washing of the water by the Word." That's why you have to have the Word preached to you. It cleanses you. The Word does the work. You just stay open and receptive. There are some things that you had that you don't have anymore. There were some negative things going on with you that left you while you were reading this book. The Word has power to liberate you when it's being preached through an anointed vessel. He said, "Faith comes by hearing and hearing by the Word of God" (Romans 10:17). Faith comes by hearing, and if your ears can't hear, you'll always be elementary in your faith. I grow because I can hear.

I keep my hands washed, so that I don't have to start in a lower dimension. It's like playing music in the wrong key. I'm in tune now, and I came back to get you in tune. God has more for you in this season, but you've got to want it. You've got to be willing to let go of yesterday and ride today into your future. Because of the disappointments and misfortunes in life, you have to wash your hands and purify your heart daily. If you shower daily, you've got to have a Word daily. When you do these things, there will be a level of worship that comes out of your being that man will never understand.

CHAPTER 5

Accommodations from on High Part 2

*So shall they fear the name of the LORD from the west,
And His glory from the rising of the sun; When the enemy
comes in like a flood, The Spirit of the LORD will lift up
a standard against him. (Isaiah 59:19, New King James
Version)*

*No temptation has overtaken you except such as is
common to man but God is faithful, who will not allow
you to be tempted beyond what you are able, but with the
temptation will also make the way of escape, that you may
be able to bear it. (1 Corinthians 10:13, New King James
Version)*

THE FLOOD ZONE

IN ISAIAH 59:19, THE LORD is saying through Isaiah
that when the enemy comes in like a flood, when
your afflictions are overflowing and causing damage,

the Lord says, "At that particular time, I will lift up a standard against the enemy." If God hasn't showed up, and He has not lifted up a standard, you have not reached the flood zone. Your problem has not reached the place where you've got to have God show up in that dimension; but if your situation has reached that place where you have to have God show up, the Spirit of the Lord is rising right now. If you need the Spirit of the Lord to raise that banner of victory over you, I'm telling you that Jehovah Nissi is all over your situation right now. When you lift your hands, the Spirit of the Lord comes in on your behalf. Tell yourself, "All my enemies are being defeated right now, not half of them, not a fourth of them but all of them."

In Exodus 17:15, we find the Israelites going up against the Amalekites. When they go up against the Amalekites, they are not skilled in war; they have been in bondage for over 400 years and they don't know anything about fighting. To make matters worse, they come in contact with a group of people who have been warring most of their lives. Moses does what he can to train the people of God for this battle that they've come into, but their victory comes because of the help of the Lord. The Spirit of the Lord begins to help them win the battle over the Amalekites. This incident is where the name Jehovah Nissi, or "Jehovah My Banner" or "the Lord My Banner," is first used in the Bible. It means you're waving the white flag of victory not defeat; the banner shows your adversary that you've got victory while you are *in* your situation. Don't wait on the situation to leave; wave your banner right now because the Spirit of God has already gotten you the victory. He's already raised the banner of victory over your life and every circumstance that seems adverse right now.

A TESTIMONY OF VICTORY

I started the church I currently pastor in a small city named Pinson, Alabama with 23 people. There were church folks, business people and entrepreneurs who thought God wasn't going to show up for me. There were people criticizing me, saying, "He ain't going to make it." They thought that because I was this little quiet guy; they didn't know the lion that was lying dormant on the inside of me. When I started waving my banner, I started driving out wolves and silencing the voices of my critics. When you start waving your banner, I don't care what they said about you or what they said wouldn't work; you need to start waving your banner and let Jehovah Nissi usher in your victory. I've already outlived their limitations on my life. I've already destroyed the box they tried to put me in. Excuse my grammar but there ain't no box; there ain't no limitation; there ain't no religion; there ain't no jurisdiction that can stop you from advancing when God is on your side. I can tell you this with assurance because my testimony is that none of these things stopped me. Jehovah Nissi raised the banner over my life just like He can and will do for you.

GET GOD INVOLVED

How much of God do you want to get involved in your situation? The bigger your problem, the bigger your praise. I don't get depressed over a problem; I just praise on another dimension. The deeper my wound, the deeper I worship; so if you've been wounded deep, then you ought to worship deep because if you haven't been wounded deep, you can't worship deep. To the measure of your pain, God will come in like a flood. If you're having a hard time dealing with the wounds, go to a deeper place in worship. Worship will activate

God to give you the answer you've been seeking. If you can take your worship to another level, that enemy that came against your life like a flood will retreat from the standard that the Spirit of the Lord will raise up. I want to activate you to a deeper level of worship. Don't put God on hold. God is now manifesting Himself. Whenever the enemy shows up like a flood, you'd better get ready for God to do something amazing. The devil and people thought if you screamed, no one would answer. Psalms 34:17 says, "The righteous cry out, and the Lord hears, And delivers them out of all their troubles." You're not going to be crying over a problem for long; you're going to have cries and tears of joy because He's turned that situation around. It's already shifted. It's already done. You're already an overcomer. You're already more than a conqueror. You're already victorious. You're already running through troops and leaping over walls. You're already in the jurisdiction that God wanted you in. It's already done. God is raising a standard.

A MINISTRY BIRTHED FROM PAIN

People don't understand that I have a ministry geared to encourage people who have been in tremendous pain, who have suffered greatly. I had to walk through hell for sixteen years just because I loved people. Now God said, "Because you walked through hell and loved people and didn't change in your heart, I'm going to give you and them ten years of unprecedented peace, favor and abundance." If you are reading this book right now, God is extending that ten years to you. If everything in your life has been smooth, you've had no problems, no pain, no unfavorable situations, then this release is not for you. But if you have felt left out, kicked to the curb, overlooked, discouraged, then this message is for you—you're the apple of God's eye. Right now, God's looking down on you and every devil that came against your life might as well get ready to exit because God's raising a standard. When God promises you a season of peace, favor and abundance, you need to start celebrating your brand new season.

WE DON'T MAKE GOOD CHURCH FOLKS

Listen: once we've entered into that season, it doesn't make sense what opportunities and help will flood your life. It doesn't make any sense at all. There are so many automatic doors that God will open for you. Continue to worship and praise him because, when you worship, as the scripture says, "deep calls unto deep." We don't make good church folks in my ministry, and I don't want you to be just a "church folk." Don't just do things in church with no real connection to God. Don't learn the ways of operating where your heart is not connected to what you do. Never allow yourself to become traditionalized where you function in the boundaries of the comfort of man. Don't just go through the motions of coming to church, lifting your hands, singing the praise and worship songs, saying "Amen" at the right time, but never reaching out to God, going after Him in worship with everything in you.

It's time to leave the "comfort zone" of religion because anytime man is comfortable, God's uncomfortable. There's something that God wants done that's not being done when man becomes comfortable; so we stay outside the perimeters of what used to be the box and we worship within the confines of God. The Word says worship Him in spirit and in truth. Everything about your worship should be true. Don't come to God half-heartedly with an agenda if you want to see Jesus manifest Himself in your life. People today are looking for the real Jesus in church. They may not be able to articulate it but they are looking for the real Jesus. The spiritual sons who are drawn to the ministry I pastor, let's just say, they ain't church boys. Some of them are straight off the street, but one day, they came into the New Birth Birmingham ministry and said, "I have to go back and whatever I have to do, if I have to stop selling drugs, if I have to stop running women, if I have to stop lying and cheating, I'll do whatever I have to do to be a part of this move of God." They are changed. Why? Because I introduced them to someone who can change them. I introduced them to the real Jesus Christ.

TEMPTATION IS COMING

First Corinthians 10:13 says, "No temptation has overtaken you except such as is common to man." So everybody has experienced everything and anything you're dealing with. Don't let the devil tell you you're an isolated case; that is not the truth. If God put it in the Word through the writing of Paul, then that is the truth. "But God is faithful, who will not allow you to be tempted beyond what you are able, but with the temptation will also make the way of escape, that you may be able to bear it." As I talk you through these things, you've got to understand, God gives you revelation of His Word for your now and your future. If you are reading this book, you may be dealing with something that's either happening right now or it's about to happen. I would make sure that whatever's about to happen, I am prepared for it. You prepare prior to so you're not reactive—you're proactive. Most of modern day Christians' lives are reactive: "I've got to get faith now that I'm in a situation." Well, get faith *before* you get in a situation. Don't start learning how to believe once something hits your life. Believe before anything ever comes into your life.

YOUR TEST IS PROOF THAT GOD IS FAITHFUL

It's common for a man to be tested to prove the faithfulness of God. It is not that God is trying to do something really special for you; God is trying to prove to you that He is faithful. One thing I understand is that God can be trusted, even when people disappoint or prove to be untrustworthy. I have a natural tendency to be trusting of people because I stay before God and He keeps me accountable to be trustworthy with others. I, then, expect that from people. I have been disappointed many times; however, even in those times when I felt like I wasn't going to be able to trust anymore, I realized that God was still faithful. I'm not standing because people have been faithful; I stand because God has been faithful. In 1 Corinthians 10:13, this common situation has come upon this man in order to prove the faithfulness of God.

A revelation that God has given me through the various dilemmas of my own life is that no matter what I've been through, somebody has already been through the same thing. Don't ever let the devil deceive you into believing lies like, "You're the only one like this," "Ain't nobody ever been treated like you've been treated," "Ain't nobody ever been talked about like you've been talked about," "Ain't nobody ever been broke," "Ain't nobody ever lost all their stuff before." Yes, they have; some gave up but some didn't. Are you going to be the one who gives up or are you going to be the one who didn't? After all is settled, are you going to be the one who has the testimony about the faithfulness of God? I will. I am not worried about what I have to walk through. I start celebrating because I know how it's going to turn out.

Listen: if I'm like the Hebrews boys, if I go through the fire, the fire is not going to burn me and you're not going to see the residue on me of what I've gone through.

There won't be any smoke in my coat after it has ended. I would have to give my testimony for you to understand I've been through hell but I didn't stop. I can say with authority that it's common for a man to be tested to prove the faithfulness of God. I cannot say for the rest of my days that I won't have a dilemma, even though I'm in ten years of unprecedented peace, favor and abundance. The devil's going to challenge that statement to see if I really believe it, just like he will challenge you about what you speak over your life. Well, it's too late; I believe that I receive and I have peace in my being, supernatural favor is on my life and you might as well get ready—you're going to see my abundance. Let that be your testimony as well. You have peace in your being, supernatural favor is on your life and you're overflowing with abundance that can't be hidden.

YOUR TEST CAN'T GET PAST YOUR FAITH

The test will never go beyond your faith capacity in God. There is no way God's going to give you a situation that you don't have the faith capacity to overcome. The scripture text confirms what I'm saying. So, where you are right now, if it is a dilemma, God believes that you have the faith capacity on the inside of you to endure whatever you're dealing with. You can look around and say this and that about your situation, but I recommend going to the Word. The Word says whatever you're dealing with right now, you have the faith capacity on the inside of you to come through that thing. You would not battle sickness in your body, if you didn't have the faith capacity to rule the sickness in your body; you would not have marital problems, if you didn't have the faith capacity to overcome the marital problems. It doesn't matter if you don't have everything together right now—you're not dead! You're still alive and you're still praising God! There is a faith capacity on the inside of you to overcome every obstacle.

Your trials and difficulties are tailor-made for your faith. How do I know? Because some problems I deal with, you wouldn't be able to deal with because I have the faith capacity to deal with my issues just like you have the faith capacity to deal with yours. I don't want to be in your situation; I want to pray for you while you're in your situation. You don't want to be in my situation; that's why you need to pray for me while I'm walking through it. In fact, we all need to pray for one another that the faith capacity on the inside of us will supersede the situations we are walking through right now.

During a training session with my leadership, the presenter gave an illustration that involved one of my administrators sitting in a chair holding a cup in each hand, arms extended to her side. As he continued with his presentation, he began to fill the cups. When he first asked for a volunteer, several people had raised their hands; however, as the illustration continued with more water being added and the strain beginning to show on the her face, I'm quite sure those volunteers were glad they weren't chosen. As I sat there, God gave me a revelation on how we look while we are walking through the tests that everyone inevitably has to face. There are some things you don't want to walk through; there are some things you may have had to close your eyes, grit your teeth and say, "Lord, if you don't send me some help, I'm not going to make it." The revelation is that the call on your life will give you the capacity to walk through things that others cannot walk through; that's why you have to make sure you're called to the places, positions and assignments that you are operating in. You don't need to get jealous of a position someone else has if you don't want to walk through the difficulties that person may be experiencing; and let me tell you, positions have problems that go along with it. Just like my administrator had a lot of weight to carry by the time the example ended, there's a weight that an individual carries based on the call on their lives. Yet, there is a capacity on the inside of you to walk through the tests for where you are called to be. You're not going to quit, you're not going to throw the towel in because what's in you determines what happens outside you. When you know people are in a difficult situation (for example they were just evicted or their children are living wild lifestyles), yet they still come to church, still praise and worship, it's because they still have the capacity to keep praising God through faith until their change comes. It's not that we all have perfect situations in our lives; there are some of us who have the capacity, even though things are a wreck, to still come in to church, open our mouths and give God glory and call Him holy when it seems like there is a hole in everything that we have. So never get jealous of somebody who's walking it out with ease—it's not easy. God just put a grace on them and a capacity to walk that thing out.

One more note on this point: there are some things that will never come your way. There are some things that will never come down your street. You want to know why? Because God has not placed that capacity on the inside of you for that challenge. You don't have to worry about that issue. Some challenges will never come in your life because God knows He has not placed the faith to withstand it on the inside of you; but whatever challenges you are facing right now, you have the wherewithal to overcome that situation. I don't care how much detail is in it; I don't care what they are saying about it; I don't care what the diagnosis is. Some people die of a lesser illness than others, but the people who live have the capacity on the inside of them. They say, "It may be hard, I'm going through chemotherapy, all my hair may be falling out, I may feel awful every day, *but* the wherewithal is on the inside of me. I can see my hair growing back; I can see muscles and weight coming back on my body; I can see myself at my business, because when I come out of this, I was an employee but now my victory over my trial is going to promote me into being an entrepreneur." When you have the wherewithal on the inside of you, you get an upgrade for every trial you make it through.

People want to know, "How in the world did Bishop Davis get into that big ole' building?" I made it through the test, that's how I got here, I made it through the test. I didn't get bitter, I got better. Anytime you can make it through the test, you are going to get better if you don't get bitter. There is something on the inside of you right now, telling you, "Don't get bitter, Don't get bitter, Don't get bitter" and you need to start speaking back, "I'm getting better, I'm getting better , I'm getting better."

YOUR TEST HAS AN ESCAPE ROUTE

The area you were about to give up in is your way of escape. The provision for escape is here for you now. You can escape the pressure, you can escape the agony and you can escape everything that the devil threatened you with. God has given you your day of escape, not Bishop Davis; I just say what God has already said. *This is your day of escape.* Escaping doesn't mean you don't have faith; escaping means that my problem didn't kill me. I can handle the weight all day long because I know when it gets too heavy, God's going to give me a way to escape. Either He's going to give me an atmosphere where I can praise beyond the pressure or He's going to give me a Word that makes me feel like I've just gotten away from my situation. If I can get away for five minutes, if I can get a break for five minutes, if I can get in a God atmosphere and just get into praise and worship for five minutes, that is an escape moment for me. If I can get a five minute break, I can run another mile. I'm reminded of Dr. King's speeches that encouraged the people not to give up during the struggle for civil rights in this country. When Dr. King stood in the pulpit of a church, he preached a message that is still relevant today. He was saying to you it's been difficult, it's been a hard ride, but there is a day of escape coming. While people were being beaten, while people were marching across the bridge at Selma, here was a man standing up and speaking the Word of God to encourage them. Today, just like then, it may be rough, but this is not the end. In fact, this is a testing point to see how determined you are.

Some of you have let up on your determination because you've been going through too many spiritual "drive through restaurants," where everything is at your finger-tips, everything is nice, everything is just like you want it so you don't have endurance anymore. A "drive through" salvation will fail you when you have to walk through an extended test. I'm glad God didn't give me that kind of salvation so when things don't happen on my timetable, I can endure till God changes my situation. Tell yourself, "It's time to escape because God is providing the ability to escape whatever is tormenting me." It doesn't torment God but, if it torments you, it moves God. Get ready, this is the day that you escape from torment.

After hearing a Word from my pastor (Apostle Eddie L. Long), I realized that it's not my situation that defeats me—it's the way I see my situation. You can keep rehearsing over and over again the things that you think are going to happen and become focused on defeat instead of victory. How many times are you going to lose your house? How many nightmares are you going to dream before you realize that God is a God of miracles? How long is it going to take you to realize that you are out of your night season? Just like I realized that I had to see my situation differently, you have to realize that your escape route from your situation will come into view when you first change how you see the life tests you're experiencing. You can keep living a nightmare when God is telling you to dream. You can keep rehearsing the dilemmas of your life when God is telling you to look toward the direction of your dream. We have a tendency to sit and go over and over and over our problems until we are emotionally tired and drained. Then, we have opened an avenue for the enemy to attack us physically because we have allowed stress and worry to steal our mental and, eventually, our physical health. You have to be careful when all you do is worry because your mind is powerful. It can release toxins in your body and tell your body it's not able to function like it should. Then your God-given assignment is jeopardized because you're not physically or mentally prepared to carry out God's plans. Today, I announce to you that you are released from that pressure; God has given you an escape route and it starts with praise. Just like David said when he was facing his challenges at Ziglag, "I'm going to encourage myself in the Lord," you should muster the strength to begin praising and worshipping God, even before your situation is resolved. There is something on the inside of you that, through the power of the Holy Ghost, will empower you to encourage yourself in the Lord. I understand the levels of pressure that are in the earth. You cannot escape those unless God be with you. It's not just in the marketplace, it's not just in society, it's in the church. If I can teach you through this book that you have a way of escape, you don't have to wait for a church service or someone to pray for you before you escape what you're going through. You can escape in one moment. If the doctor gives me a bad report today, my hands will go up and my heart will be lifted up toward God and I will escape that very moment. Another scripture says, "Greater is He who lives in me than he who lives in the world." The ability to overcome is on the inside of *you*.

YOU WILL OVERCOME

In His Word, God promised whatever common thing you've got going on, someone else has already experienced it. Let me encourage you with this message: you will overcome in every situation. I have discovered that anything I face on my journey, it's because God placed it there to prove something to me. Again, anything I endure on my journey, God placed it there to prove something to me. Anything that you experience while you're on your journey, God placed it there to prove something to you, which means that whatever you face on your journey, you can go ahead and start celebrating right in the middle of it. You want to know why? You're destined to come out on the other end of it. Keep trusting in the Lord. Don't allow yourself to get distant from God and start trusting in something that can't hold you up. Realize that God will get you through everything you are going to deal with in life. The Red Sea did not split because Moses lifted the rod; the Red Sea split because Moses believed in the God that had the power over the Red Sea. I want to tell you right now that if you would just keep responding to God, keep trusting in Him, keep praising and worshipping Him, God will make your situations respond as well. It is faith on the inside of you that will get you through everything you have to walk through in this lifetime. If you keep operating by faith in God, the obstacles in your way are about to move; the mountains you are going to speak to are going to be cast into the sea; things that have been tormenting you, you are about to torment right now; things that have been trying to override you and overthrow you, you are about to overthrow. Whatever it is, it does not have victory over you. You are an overcomer.

Let's pray: Father, I bless you, I honor you, I thank you for this time of study and advancement. God, I give you all the glory, honor and praise for what you've already done. I'm not waiting to see it before I praise you. I already know that by faith everything that you have preordained for my life and others is already done, Amen.

CHAPTER 6

We Must Enter Into His Rest

Therefore, since a promise remains of entering His rest, let us fear lest any of you seem to have come short of it. For indeed the gospel was preached to us as well as to them; but the word which they heard did not profit them, not being mixed with faith in those who heard it. For we who have believed do enter that rest, as He has said: "So I swore in My wrath, 'They shall not enter My rest,' " although the works were finished from the foundation of the world. For He has spoken in a certain place of the seventh day in this way: "And God rested on the seventh day from all His works"; and again in this place: "They shall not enter My rest." Since therefore it remains that some must enter it, and those to whom it was first preached did not enter because of disobedience, again He designates a certain day, saying in David, "Today," after such a long time, as it has been said: "Today, if you will hear His voice, Do not harden your hearts." For if Joshua had given them rest, then He would not afterward have spoken of another day. There remains therefore a rest for

the people of God. For he who has entered His rest has
himself also ceased from his works as God did from His.
(Hebrews 4: 1–10, New King James Version)

THE REST REMAINS

One of the words that is key in this passage of scripture is "remain." I want to give you the definition of the word because it's very important for people to understand its meaning as they move toward a certain destination or location. If they don't believe that what was promised to be at that destination still exists, they often feel as though they deprived themselves for nothing or will not obey in that area at all. "Remain" means "to continue in the same state." It also means "to be left after removal, loss, destruction of an item." So when God says a rest remains, it doesn't matter what happens, it's still in the same state as when it was first promised to someone. Regardless of what is removed, that rest is still in the same state. Regardless of what anyone says or if they cause loss in some way, the rest remains in the same state. Regardless of what destruction, what tsunami of challenges comes, the rest is still in the same state. The problem is not that the rest no longer exists; it does. Our problem is just like the children of Israel's problem—we can't obey long enough to get that rest. No, don't try to rewrite the Bible, the rest still remains—it is our obedience that's not intact. God said it several times: it remains, it remains, it remains. When God made this statement about the children of Israel not entering His rest, He was referring to everyone, even Joshua. They entered into the promise but not the rest, which means they got money but they didn't get rest; they got the house but they didn't have rest; they drive the car but they don't have rest. You can get all the stuff but you've got to have rest to go along with what you have. In this season, you don't have to pursue more stuff; it will come to you automatically if you are connected to a house where there is rest. The Bible says in Deuteronomy 28 that the blessings will run you down and overtake you (**v. 2).** So the blessing is not the problem; obedience is the problem.

DISOBEDIENCE CANCELS OUT YOUR REST

Consistent obedience will always bring about a tremendous blessing but also a blessing of peace. However, the problem from the very beginning has been disobedience. Adam became the first reluctant example of what happens to your rest when you operate in disobedience. The problem wasn't that he didn't have access to rest, peace, favor, abundance; the problem was he didn't know how to do what God told him to do. God said, "You can have access to everything but that tree in the midst of the garden, don't touch it, that's not yours, I've reserved that, don't touch that." So Adam is now coerced by another voice that causes him to do what God told him not to do. When you do what God tells you not to do, you come into a place called disobedience and it blocks you out of that place that God has designated as a rest day for you. So we have a lot of people in church who are looking for rest. Well, rest is directly attached to obedience, so from the beginning, I learned some principles about obedience.

People don't like what I do but they can't stop what I do because what I do is birthed out of obedience. I didn't do it because the trustee board said I could; I did it because the Word told me to do it and that's called obedience. Once I come to the knowledge of the truth and then refuse it, it's disobedience. It is wrong for me to expect to have a blessing with rest and not be in obedience. I may have the blessing but I won't have the rest. I will always worry about someone stealing what God gave me; that is not rest. If I'm standing at the window with a pistol in my hand, looking out the window all the time, trying to protect what God gave me, this is not rest. If I'm staying up all night, worrying about my child when God said the fruit of my (wife's) womb is blessed, that is not rest. God has designated rest for us.

God gave me this statement one time and I keep it in the front of my Bible as a constant reminder. He said, "Your understanding can wait but your obedience cannot." When God gives you a command, if you wait until you understand it from every angle, your opportunity has already gone. If you're waiting to obey when you have complete understanding, your day of peace and rest has already departed.

Consider windows and doors. Both represent opportunity; a window is a term we use for a limited time of opportunity. It is not something that is always going to be open. So some of you thought it was a door, which represents an opportunity that stays open. Windows don't open as wide as doors, and windows are open for a limited amount of time; that's why you can't play around with disobedient people when there is a window of opportunity. Some people say, "Well, I think we need to have another meeting about this," "I believe we need to talk about this." I believe we need to obey. I believe we need to do exactly what God says because on the other side of that window that we are squeezing through is ten years of unprecedented peace, favor and abundance—the best days of your life are here right now.

For some people, your window may open despite your age. You may come out of retirement into a new assignment from God. Don't say, "Not me." You don't understand, the Bible says He renews our youth like the eagle. When you are about to hit the ground, all of a sudden your wings gain more strength because you are now in that season of rest. If He calls you to go through a window, He will give you the strength, health and vitality to accomplish the task.

I have been checking something out for years now. I've been watching and monitoring the various gospel preachers and teachers who come on Christian television. I've been monitoring their health, activities, even the way they dress, and they seem to look younger each year, almost as if they are aging in reverse. They look healthy, rested, peaceful and focused. You want to know why? They didn't miss their promise. So, I focus in on that type of the thing because I don't want to get old before I get old. I have a lot God wants me to accomplish. When you get in a certain mode of worrying and complaining, you start aging faster. However, when you enter into the rest of God, it's like rolling back some time.

What you don't understand is that the thing you've been worried about has kept you from that place He calls rest. He designated a time of rest for us. I received a Facebook message from one of my spiritual sons who lives in Atlanta. He had seen a recent picture of me and, in the message, he said, "Man, you look like you about 25."

I said, "Sho nuff, show you right, say it again." There is a thing that happens when you enter into His rest; they can't tell what age you are. I feel better today than when I was actually 25. You want to know why? It's because I'm in rest and I'm going to stay in rest. I'm going to keep obeying God, and God is going to keep refreshing me. It doesn't matter what's going on around me; I'm in my place of rest. They have been talking about this fountain of youth; let me tell you where it is: in His rest. For some of you, the aches are leaving right now, the pains are leaving and the cartilages are coming back right now. You want to know why? We're moving you to where you should have been all along. Nobody wants to be a part of something dying; everybody wants to be a part of something living. As you read this book, you're in rest; you're in ten years of unprecedented peace, favor and abundance.

REST REQUIRES OBEDIENCE

So, God said the promised rest remains; it has not been entered into. All those years have passed and it still remains. That means everything those people were going after, they missed it. In your lifetime, you could have been tied to somebody who missed it. They were after it. They knew it exists but didn't know how to get to it. The scripture says they didn't enter in because of disobedience. The key to the door where the rest "remains" is obedience. I don't care how much you have disobeyed prior to this day, all you have to do is repent and say, "God, whatever you say, from this day forward , I'm going to do what you said, because I'm not going to be locked out of something that you have promised me I can have if I just obey you."

People struggle with this thing called obedience. You shouldn't. You've got to tap into the nature that's beyond your time in this earth. You existed long before your birthday. This isn't deep; you existed before your birthday. The "you" that wasn't in this world obeyed God. The reason you have to be born again is that when you were born into this world, you were shaped in iniquity. When you get born again, now we're reshaping you back into God's original plan for your life. So what did God say about you originally? You wouldn't be in the projects now; you wouldn't have been raised in the projects; you wouldn't have been in some low-income housing or depending on governmental help. That wasn't God's original plan for you. So God talks through His original plan concerning you; you listen through all the pain, hurt, discouragement and rejections that you've experienced since you have been in this earth. I assure you that you weren't talking about who hurt you on that side where your spirit was with God because nobody could hurt you on that side. When we get you back into rest, it doesn't matter what they do, they can't hurt you. When you choose to obey, you don't fluctuate anymore. I've been practicing this thing, which is why I don't fluctuate financially and I don't fluctuate in assets. Why? Because I learned to obey. I'd have to disobey, in some area of my life, in order to fluctuate. I didn't say I don't have challenges; I said I don't fluctuate. If you follow the pattern I have learned and practice in my everyday life, you won't fluctuate either.

Some people fluctuate with obedience because they have had bad examples or they have been taught incorrectly about what God requires. I was counseling with a preacher one day, trying to give him some guidance concerning his ministry. He began to tell me how he was a part of an association that had certain practices, especially when they went to conventions, that everyone was expected to participate in. He told me that he learned to do what they were doing. I told him, "When you are involved with those type of organizations that teach you disobedience instead of obedience, you have to be cleansed of the teachings and practices." Those faulty examples of godly living work directly against your rest and you'll wonder what's wrong. Even if you are a church member, you may have been operating under faulty teaching and you're thinking, "I've been going to church all my life and ain't nothing happened." You want to know why? Some place in your life, there is some disobedience. Once you find and locate that area of disobedience, then what you do is get some Word, get some prayer and get some worship. Begin to infiltrate those areas with the Word of God, prayer and worship. If you have to look in the mirror and talk to your flesh, tell it, "Listen here, I'm deputized to tell you that you're not going to go over to his house anymore. You're not going over to her house late at night anymore."

During a two-week period, I was running into people who used to attend the church that owned the building prior to our ministry. One Wednesday night, I met a woman who said she grew up in the church. About two days later, I met another guy who said he had grown up in this same church. A few days after that, I met a guy who also grew up in the same church. He started talking about the disobedience that brought the house down. He said, "We were booming. This was the largest church in Birmingham." He explained how all the major crusades took place in our building. Despite such height in the ministry, disobedience among the leaders caused the house to fall apart. People began to leave in droves; fifty families left at one time.

Disobedience, especially among leadership, will always bring a downfall to ministry and to people's lives. The impact of disobedience is treacherous. Somebody is always going to pay when there is disobedience. That person may have pleasure for a moment but somebody connected to him or her is going to experience loss, naturally or spiritually.

So, this rest was promised and never accessed. In the region where I live, I know that people have not experienced this rest I am referring to, even within the church. Too many people come to church, looking troubled, weighed down and worried. No, people at rest do not carry that type of load. What's in your mind, weighing down your praise? You don't have to worry like that. You don't have to be down like that. God hooked you up before the foundation of the world. He saw this day back in the Creation and He knew the people who are walking the earth today were going to need the rest He was establishing. Not a pretend rest, but a real rest. God knew at one point and time in your life that you were going to need a break. You've been worried about bills; you've been worried about people; you've been worried about things; you've been worried about *everything*.

So God said, "I'm going to send you ten years of unprecedented peace, favor and abundance. I'm going to give you ten years to get that load off your back. I'm going to give you ten years to teach you how to not carry things that you should be walking on."

Let me teach you something I've learned from experience. Some things you encounter, you just need to say, "So what!" Yeah, if they say they don't want to be your friend anymore, so what! It doesn't matter.

But some things do matter. Some moments are truly difficult. Tragedy strikes or you lose a loved one. Yet a difficult moment is still only a moment. You don't have to keep living it. I have had tragic moments of loss and disappointment. But if I can get past those moments, I can still live a lifetime of peace and rest. I don't have to stay in that painful moment. If God said He had a rest for me, right after that moment, I'm going to find that rest through my obedience. I'm not going to be discouraged; I'm not going to be a grieving leader; I am going to enter into that rest. Let your problem drive you into the rest of God.

PURSUE THE REST OF GOD

If you're not pursuing the rest of God, you're not in enough pain. You are still using some painkillers. That is the only reason you haven't entered in; you've got something to medicate yourself and that's why you're coping with this terrible moment you've been living in for the past few days, weeks or even years. People talk; someone will say, "Well, Pastor, it's been bad, it's real been bad." Well, why aren't you pursuing the rest of God? Because if it's been that bad, you should run after this rest I've been talking about like a marathon sprinter. If my hand gets burnt, I'm going to take it off the heater, I'm going to take it out the fire. I'm not going to leave my hand in something that's causing me pain.

God promised them a rest because He knew life was painful. I can imagine God saying, "This is what I'm going to do. I have a day called the Sabbath Day; it's when I stop everything and chill. What I'm going to do for you, I'm not just going to give you a day, I'm going to create a place where you can just chill, where you don't have anything to worry about." Yeah, she left but it's all right; what's coming is better than what left you. Yeah, you lost it, but now you have room for the thing God is bringing, because now you are going to need two places where you had a spot for one.

Jabez said, "Enlarge my territory." He knew what it was like to be in pain and to cause pain; he said, "Enlarge my territory," because there is something coming behind this that is bigger than whatever existed before this. I stay excited because I recognize that every day God is doing something greater and greater in my life. I'm up early in the morning, excited; I don't get up griping, I get up excited. "Look at what the Lord has done. This is the day that the Lord has made. We can rejoice and be glad in it."

If He gives me another day, He gives me another opportunity to rejoice in the Lord and again, I say, rejoice. Someone is saying, "Well, preacher, I don't see how we can get there." Well, close your eyes and then you'll see it because it's a dream, but with God, dreams come to pass. You've been living that nightmare with your eyes open. Well, I just made up my mind: if God had a place for me like a dream, I'm going to live in it. Call me crazy but you've got to call me blessed at the same time.

Some of you are afraid of what people will say about you but what they think about you doesn't mean anything. Does that change anything just because they think it? It can't change you and it hasn't changed them for the better. You've got to get rid of some of that trashy thinking before God can change your situation. People who think evil of you are evil anyway so why are you worried about it? Good people think good things about people. I think everybody's for me because I'm for whatever I'm a part of.

When you start living these ten years, you are not going to come to church wondering who's out to get you. You're not going to realize that sister was trying to do something to hurt you when she promoted you. Sometimes people try to put you in a positive place to embarrass you. For some of you, they didn't put you in a negative place, they put you in a positive place because they thought you were going to be ashamed. All of a sudden, they put you in the right place and you got promoted. All of a sudden, the leader says, "Where you been? I've been looking for you the last six months." Some tripped out usher brought you to the front seats and said, "Those seats are reserved seats but we are going to sit you here." You thought it was a setup to fail but it turned into a good thing because the pastor was looking for you to carry out an assignment he had in mind. Now, you're more connected than ever; what was meant to be embarrassing has turned into a blessing. You got positioned on purpose.

DON'T FOLLOW SATAN'S EXAMPLE

Obedience is everything. It's the thing that the devil cannot do; the devil cannot obey. This was his problem in Heaven and it is still his problem today. It's his greatest weakness; he cannot do what God tells him to do. You have to do the opposite of Satan.

People talk about spiritual warfare. You know how Jesus overcame spiritual warfare? With obedience. Everything the Father told Him to do, He did, and the devil didn't have any power over Him. The very time that I feel like that there is something huge coming my way that will be negative for my life, I line myself up with a little more obedience. At my church, we fast the first three days of every month. When I hear something bad, get a negative report or have to deal with some adverse situation, I don't go fast, I've already fasted. I line myself up to obey. So I find what the order is from God and I obey it. When I obey it, it breaks all the curses; they just fall to the ground. What doesn't fall to the ground boomerangs back to the sender. Obedience is so powerful that all the witches collected together in the region can't stop you with their curses. Once you get in this place, nothing else can have impact on you in a negative way. Once you obey, you're unstoppable.

There are things I don't worry about at all. Why? If I have done my part in obedience, God's going to do His part. God is faithful to those who will obey Him. Try this test. Take one week and just do what the Word of God tells you to do and watch demons run screaming. When I talk about demons, I'm talking about depression; I'm talking about low self-esteem; I'm talking about pain; I'm talking about discomfort; I'm talking about financial issues; I'm talking about marital issues. They can't handle obedience. Your rest is one step of obedience away—one step.

The Bible is supposed to be taught, and then you're supposed to be taught obedience to the Word you have heard. When leaders teach people how to benefit through obedience, you're going to always be sustained. If your supervisor says, "Well, we're terminating you at the end of the week," then you say, "Well, either I'm getting a promotion or I'm about to open up my own business because what you said doesn't scare me at all. I've been obeying God, so it's not going to affect me in a negative way."

I have so much confidence in obedience, I do it every day. Whatever you have confidence in, you do it on a consistent basis. It's not that bad things haven't happened; they just didn't have an impact on me. Obedience can keep bad things from having an impact on you. If you've been diagnosed with something terminal, you need to say to God, "God, what would you have me to do? What area of obedience do I need to act on in my life?" Tell God, "No matter what the report might say, death cannot overthrow your purpose in me." Hear me, death may be able to overrule you but it can't overrule God's purpose in you. The more that things come against you, the more you need to get in God's purpose and obey what He tells you to do.

God may wake you up one morning and tell you to call someone and reconcile the relationship. I don't care if you have one eye open and the other eye shut, pick up the phone and call the person God told you to call. Find a way to obey God. Don't let anybody talk you out of it. You're only going to seem like a fool for a moment; remember, a moment is only a short space of time. They thought I was a fool, too, but "How you like me now?" You're about to say to them, "How you like me now?" through your obedience. Your obedience is sealing your destiny right now. What you do today in your obedience, I promise you, will prevent the devil from stealing what he's trying to steal from you. Everything that tried to curse you can't curse you; everything that tried to eat up your harvest has got to shut its mouth right now.

OBEDIENCE WITHSTANDS THE CIRCUMSTANCES

Throughout the Bible, we see examples of obedience by individuals who received extraordinary deliverances. I like Shadrach, Meshach and Abednego. These weren't their real names. Their captors gave them new names in order to maintain a certain bondage mindset.

Yet, they didn't respond like captives. When faced with bowing to idolatry or standing for what they believed, they acknowledged the authority of the king but also let him know they would not bow to the image. In other words, they would not disobey God by worshipping something else. They said, "We're not bowing and because we're not bowing, when you throw us in the fire, even if we perish, we're still not going to serve your god."

Listen, even if I ain't got nothing but five people in this big old building God gave me, I'm still not going to serve a religious god. I'm still not going to go over into traditional ways of operating. Shadrach, Meshach and Abednego made it clear that even if God didn't deliver them, they still were not going along with the status quo.

When they are thrown into the fiery furnace, the heat is so intense, it consumes the men who throw them in. They are now in the fire but the obedience to God doesn't allow them to burn. Their obedience is more powerful than the elements.

Now, you tell me, how can cancer kill you when fire couldn't burn them when they were obeying? "Doctor, I know what you diagnosed me with, but you don't know how obedient I am." So what used to stick to me just slides right off.

Then, we see this guy named Daniel whom they throw in the lions' den with hungry lions. These weren't lions that had a meal yesterday or earlier that morning. The Bible describes the lions as ferocious. Even though the lions were hungry, Daniel's obedience would not allow them to consume him. He had been obedient despite the threats of the enemy. "Don't you dare swing that window open and pray anymore. You cannot pray to your God."

Daniel said, "To not pray to my God would be disobedience. You can change every law in this city, but if it conflicts with the Word of God, I'm not with it. I will not obey any law that violates God's law. Anything that conflicts with the Word of God will violate my protective covering if I obey it rather than Him.

So, Daniel is now in with the hungry lions but because of his obedience, they lose their appetite.

There are some things that you knew were threatening that are about to become your friend. In this season, biblically speaking, your enemies are going to be at peace with you. If you can embrace this, there is no need to stay up talking about this with your prayer partner. As a matter of fact, you and your prayer partner are not going to have anything to talk about anymore. There is going to be a major gap of silence on the next phone call. You want to know why? Because you're not going to be able to talk about what your haters are doing. Your haters are about to love you and not know why. It's hard for the mind to believe this, but if you can't believe this with the mind, you have to believe it with your heart.

OBEDIENCE IS A HEART THING

Everything in God is a heart thing, not a mind thing. He already knows your mind is jacked up. You've been hurt too much by people and it hurts you emotionally, so God already knows your mind can't handle the things of God. The question is, can your heart handle what I'm saying? The Bible says, "Harden not your heart." He's saying don't resist this message you are reading because, if you resist it, it can't happen. So God says, "Harden not your heart. Don't resist what's being read right now because many people may read this book, but if you resist its message, it can't come to pass and it makes Me (God) look bad." You want to know why God's looking bad? Because we've been resisting what He's been saying. You want to know why people don't believe in our God? Because we resist Him and it shows in every area of our lives. Our hearts are hard. Our hearts are callous against God; so what He says, we don't believe it. People are looking at us, shouting and running, attending church on a regular basis and we don't have what God promised.

You're about to have it, and everyone is going to see it. I tell people all the time they're not intelligent when the Word of God is being preached and they're resisting. That is not intelligence; it is just the opposite. That is foolishness, especially when you know you've got a crisis. When you have a crisis, you need a Word or you're going to stay in crisis because crisis is only ended by a Word from the Lord. God lead you to this book not only to give you a Word concerning your crisis, but also to get you out of your crisis so that you can go free and enjoy your rest.

If your rest is close to you, why would you stay in crisis by not receiving the Word of the Lord? I would do whatever I needed to do; I would tell my head, "Shut up, while I open up my heart so I can receive the Word of the Lord because I'm ready to get out of a crisis."

GOD IS VALIDATED WHEN YOU REST

We must enter into His rest. Listen, you want to know what validates God's existence? You. *You* validate the Word of God. What He said is validated by its manifestation in you. Some of you might be thinking I'm talking about money. God is not just increasing you financially but He's getting you over into the exceedingly, abundantly all you can ask or think. But first, I'm talking about your heart and getting this Word that's sharper than any double-edged sword into your life. The Bible says it's a discerner of the heart, the intent of the heart. I need this Word to get in your heart so God can get you some abundance; then, offering time is not a struggle, paying your bills is not a struggle, taking care of your children's expenses are not a problem. If there is a small crack in your heart, that crack is allowing truth to get into your heart; you can truly discern who your man or woman of God is and how he or she is trying to help you get to where God wants you to be. Turn off your head for a moment and let your heart receive what I'm telling you. If you turn your head back on, you're going to turn your heart back off and it's going to keep you locked up for the next fifteen years. There is no reason to get jealous of people who are now in rest. No, you have an opportunity, based on the revelation of what God is saying through His *logos*, to enter into rest. His logos says He has a rest; the revelation is: it's for you. Hear me, if the logos, which is the written Word of God, says there is a rest, the revelation of it says it's for me. If

I was you, I wouldn't be disconnected from the man or woman of God during this season. Put your hand on your chest right now and repeat these words, "It's for me. Rest is for me." If you think you've already arrived, watch my brother and sister around you maximize in this season, and it's going to make you start moving, make you start believing, make you start praising. You're going to stop wondering why they are running around the church because there's some stuff that's going to happen to you that's going to make you run around your neighborhood and you're not going to have on jogging clothes.

IT'S TIME

It's time, it's time, it's time! All God needs is someone who will believe to the point of obedience. People may ask you why you are withdrawing from something. You can say, "Because God has a higher purpose for me and I'm not going to stay here and let this define me. I am already defined by God."

Do you want to come out of what you're in and enter into His rest? Jesus said to the man who had been at the pool of Bethesda for so long, "Do you want to come out?"

The man started telling him about all the situations that had been going on, "Every time I try to get in the pool, somebody gets in before me." He starts rehearsing all that he had been through.

Jesus looks at him and says, "Do you want to be healed? Do you want to come out or do you want to keep complaining?" He has to ask him a question; he has to make him think, "Do you want to be healed? Do you want to be whole? Do you want to have finances? Do you want to have peace in your marriage? Do you want it? Because we've got to understand something here, if you don't want it, there's nothing I can do for you. Do you want it?"

Because when you really want it, no one can stop you from getting it, not in a season like this. If you believe that you receive and you want it, celebrate like it's already done. It's been done for over two thousand years and now it's been sealed. The devil's never been able to steal it; he's never been able to move it, so he knew that it was solid. Instead of moving the rest, he moved us; he blinded us; he confused us. Because he could not do anything with it, he crosses up your mind so you can't recognize it, even if you are looking at it. The devil wants to make us so immature that we don't know right from wrong. So we call good evil and evil good because if we ever get a revelation of what's already done, nothing for the next several generations will be able to stop us.

Somebody said, "Well, I thought Jesus was coming back." Well, if Jesus doesn't come back for three generations, I'm still going to be okay. I believe that everything is seasonal, on point but you have to be ready. The Bible says the scales fell from their eyes. There's something that the enemy doesn't want you to see, but he can't get rid of it. He can blind the people who are supposed to see it, he can make your ears dull of hearing, but he can't get rid of it. The enemy doesn't want you to hear, wants you to struggle with a profitable message, tailored for you. But you can say, "Not today devil, not today. What I've received today from this book, hell can't take it away."

So right now, God is opening up your eyes to see. He's enlarging your territory and increasing your capacity to believe and obey. Obedience never cancels destiny but it enlarges the perimeter of what God has already commanded toward you. Right now, some things are unraveling and untangling so you can extend yourself to believe and obey. We must enter this rest, so believe that the rest remains, you're positioned to enter into it and you'll operate in obedience to see the manifestation. It is time.

WE MUST ENTER HIS REST PART 2

I'm going to show you how strategic the enemy has been to try to keep you outside of the rest God promised. To review what I've covered concerning entering His rest, we know:

1. You have to believe for your rest.

2. Disobedience keeps you locked out of your rest.

3. It is important that you hear and receive. Hearing is not good enough; you have to hear and receive. Let me tack something else onto the chain: if you hear and you receive, you shall conceive. Our problem is conception. You heard, you say you received, but you're not showing any evidence. If you receive, then you're going to be pregnant with something.

4. The rest is not taken away or used up. There is no way the promise of God can be taken away or removed or used up.

5. Our obedience, pure obedience, will give us rest. People say Jesus whipped the devil with all power; Jesus whipped the devil with obedience. He would not go outside of what God told him to do or say.

Using Hebrews 4:1–10, let's look at some other points that will help you stay focused so that you can enter this rest.

FOCUS ON THE REST

Stay focused. Focus is very, very important when you get this close. The closer you get, the more focused you have to become. You need to start focusing from the very beginning, but the closer you get, the more focused you have to become. Satan doesn't get intimidated until you get close. Some people are always talking about "the devil's fighting me." The devil isn't fighting you because you aren't close enough. The closer you get to understanding and embracing what God has for you, the more things will kick up. The more things that will come into your life as a distraction because you are so close. The distractions are only an announcement to you that you are closer than you've ever been. Don't get upset because stuff's flying around; just don't go with it. When things became turbulent, I make sure I stay focused. I don't care what's flying around, what's turning and twisting; I'm the set man of the house, so I can't fly off like that. I can't just go off and say I'm going to be in depression for about a week. I can't do that, not on this level. You should be the same. I'm canceling the enemy's assignment to have you sitting around, depressed, bitter and angry. You're too close to your rest to let some temporary disturbances throw you off course. Tell yourself, "I'm real close to what God promised me."

ARE WE THERE YET?

Some people want you to believe that we've already entered into this rest that I'm talking about. These things will help us to better understand when we have.

1. If we are still living under the traditions of men—separation, hatred, competition and jealousy—we are not there yet.

2. There is a test of obedience before entering into every new dimension of a rest, restful life.

3. This is a corporate obedience.

113

4. A single person's imperfections should be corrected internally while the Body continues to move toward the promise.

5. Never let internal imperfections cancel your promise.

6. Now that you have the evidence, you should measure how close you are.

TRADITIONS OF MEN DELAY YOUR REST

If we are still living under the traditions of men that make the Word of God of none effect, we have not entered into rest. It's going to take a Word to get you in there. So the traditions of men work directly against the Word of God. What are the traditions of men? Attitudes that say, "Let's do it this way; why don't we do it this way?" I say, "Why don't we do it the way the Bible says to do it?" So the traditions of men make the Word of God of none effect. Separation is a big issue within the Body of Christ. It's hard to get people to come together.

There is an anointing on me that was prophesied over me in California that I would bring unity to the region I live in, but people work so hard to be separate. When you are separate, you are alone and out there by yourself. When you fall, you have no one to lift you up. That means that if it's cold, you have no one to warm you. The book of Ecclesiastes says, "a three-fold cord is not easily broken." If you're not bonded or knitted together with somebody and you get in trouble, you're going to lose out completely. You should look for those who are yoked to God's Word and the Body of Christ like you are yoked, people who believe like you believe. It's not based on whether they are loud or quiet; it's not whether they preach or teach; it's the faith that they have to believe in what God has promised. That's the kind of thing that I'm drawn to and you should be drawn to as well. So if there are traditions of men, there is separation. Wherever there is hatred, there is also competition. You can't compete with a brother or sister in Christ who's got the same blood of Jesus covering him or her that you have covering you. You don't compete with people. I'm not competing with another church; I'm not competing with another pastor; I just do what I'm called to do. Ain't nobody in my lane. What am I going to compete for? They can't take my prize. The race is not given to the swift, nor the strong but to he who endureth to the end. I'm just trying to hang in here.

So, I'm not competing with anyone because if I'm last, I get it. It's not how fast and strong that I am; it's about my endurance. I can hang in during my worst day. I can keep on moving whether I'm in a sprint or crawling. All they are going to be able to say about me is "He never gave up." I'm not in competition; I'm not jealous of anybody because I don't want what they have. Jealousy is stimulated when you want what somebody else has and you always want what somebody else has when you don't know what God has given you. When you know what God has given you, you're not jealous of what somebody else has. I am not jealous of what various pastors in this region have because I know what God gave me to be a steward over. I just enjoy what God gave me and I say, "God, just give me more of what you're going to give me." Amen.

A TEST, THEN REST

There is a test of obedience before entering into every new dimension of restful life. Some of you know that before you move to the next place, there is always some type of test. If you attended school, moved to another position within a company or achieved some goal, you know a test was required before you moved to that level. It doesn't mean the test came from God, but there's always some kind of "exam" that is going to test your obedience. Let me give you an example from the Word to validate this point. In Numbers 14, God gave the people a test. In this passage, the people had been promised that God was going to do something amazing. God was going to lead them into the Promised Land. He instructed Moses to send in twelve spies to survey the land. Ten of them came back with a negative report; two came back and said "We are well able."

Well, God told them to go in, so the test was—will you go in? There were giants in the land, the sons of Anak were there, but God was testing them to see if they would obey. Today, God is still asking the question —will you still go in, even though there are things in your promise that seem intimidating? God will never send you into something that doesn't have something on the inside that seems intimidating. The test is, will you move on the Word of God or will you go by what you see? The test is, will you do what God said or will you go by what you see? If you go by what you see, you're going to be like those other ten gentlemen who were heads of households; these were the leaders of that day. They stayed outside and stirred up the people in doubt and unbelief. There were two who believed God in spite of what they had seen.

Listen to what Caleb said in Numbers 14: 9: "Only do not rebel against the Lord, nor fear the people of the land, for they are our bread." Yeah, the people you are afraid of are your lunch. Then Caleb said, "Their protection has departed from them, and the Lord is with us." This is a powerful revelation that Caleb had versus what the other ten spies believed. Caleb was telling the people that there was no help for the giants in the Land, because God was with the Israelites. In other words, Caleb was saying, "Man, why you sitting there like that? They don't even have any protection anymore and you got God with you. Why are you waiting to respond?" In the scripture text, Caleb told them, "Do not rebel." That means God told you what to do and you said "No." It would be different if God didn't tell you anything, but if God tells you something, He expects obedience.

God is not expecting you to start talking about everything you don't have because He says, "I am." He says, "I am Jehovah Jireh, I am the Provider," so why are you sitting there talking about what you don't have? He said, "I Am." Whatever you try to say you don't have, He says, "I Am." Whatever excuse you come up with, He says, "I Am." Moses tried to say, "Well, who shall I say sent me?" God said, "Tell them I Am sent you. I Am a snake if you need me to be a snake; I Am a staff if you need me to be a staff; I Am locusts; I Am flies; I Am everything that you need me to be when you need me to be it, so stop talking about what they have and what they're doing and do what I said."

This has been a problem. We've not obeyed because we've gone through a few challenges that only made us better. I came from 23 people in a storefront building to over 93,000 square feet of property and I'm still expanding. Don't think for one minute that I haven't had any challenges. Challenges are my motivation. If I don't have a challenge, I feel like I'm dead. The only people who don't have challenges are in the grave. As long as I have a challenge, I know that I'm still alive; as long as I've got some type of challenge, I know I'm still in ministry. When you're in ministry and you stop having challenges, that's a sign to you that you may be *in* ministry, but you're not *doing* ministry because ministry brings about challenges. Anytime you try to liberate, teach or educate people, there are going to be some challenges. So, I don't mind having the challenges; I don't mind having Tobiah and his cohorts trying to talk me down from my assignment and get me off focus. I've got scripture that tells me what to do when they come. You can't stop me, Gesham, because I've come too far and seen too much to stop now. When you are a mover and a shaker, things shake all the time. You have to become comfortable with stuff that shakes every once and a while. You just keep on moving. If you get this down in your spirit, everything that God had as a dream, it's manifestation time right now. You've been scared of the shakes and the shakes are just a sign that you're accelerating. Everything shakes when it's starts accelerating. So you're going to have a few challenges, but these are things that we must identify and know how to handle when they come. We have to deal with them properly, overcome them and keep moving.

CORPORATE OBEDIENCE BRINGS REST

This is a corporate obedience. When God spoke to leaders in the Bible, He was speaking to all the children of Israel. When God talked to Moses, He was talking to all of them; it's a corporate obedience that He expected. He is now speaking to the Body of Christ, so it's a corporate obedience and not based on the act of a single person's imperfections. Let me tell you what that means - people have imperfections. You're only going to get perfection through a corporate body. You cannot get perfection through a single individual. He or she is not built to be perfect; it is the coming together as the Body that makes us perfect. As long as you function as a single individual, disjointed, removed from the principles of God, you will never fulfill God's purpose for your life. It takes all of us to obey Him. Those of you who think you are insignificant, that is not the truth; you are significant. It takes all of us. You may not be have a leadership position in the ministry, but it takes you. Your church needs your energy in the atmosphere. When you're not there, they feel the deficit in the atmosphere. When you come into your church's sanctuary, you add your agreement to the atmosphere when you believe that you receive. Now everyone begins to receive because we are united in our faith. So, it's not the single imperfections of an individual that stops us because we are a corporate body. We're all joined together. When God speaks to New Birth Birmingham, He is not just talking to Bishop Stephen Davis; He is speaking to every member connected to the ministry. When God speaks to your man or woman of God, He is speaking to you too. Don't get the attitude that says, "Let him go do it." No, God's talking to all of us. If God is talking to all of us, then He expects all of us to respond.

FIX IT AND KEEP MOVING

A single person's imperfections should be corrected internally while the Body continues to move toward the promise. When there is an issue with an individual, we, the church, cease our movement. Everything is now focused on that individual that has an imperfection, so the whole church has now taken its eyes off the promise. You know how people start gossiping, "Girl, I didn't hear that," and you're Facebooking and telling people about things that are negative; the whole church becomes focused on a single imperfection in the Body instead of remaining on track with the promise. At that point, the church is no longer focused in on the promise. It has taken its attention off the promise and soon, the movement stops. In Numbers 12, Moses' sister, Miriam, opposes the leadership of her brother and is struck with leprosy.

119

The whole camp had to stop for seven days. People were probably saying, "Aw, what are we going to do about Miriam?" or "How are we going to help Miriam?" or "Aw, she shouldn't have done it." People will talk in different ways, but all of them are focused in on this one individual. Now, the whole church is no longer even thinking about the promise. They're not even echoing the sermon about the promise; everybody is now focused in on this one imperfection going on in the church. Nobody is talking about the blessing anymore; everybody is talking about a weakness in an individual in the church.

The whole church is in the ditch and getting further and further away from the promise because everybody is focused in on the weakness of an individual. It seems as though we like to talk about stuff that is weak more than we like to talk about stuff that is strong. Now everything's catering to this individual and his or her weakness instead of handing it over to the ministry so they can keep on moving. You must learn how to handle situations appropriately and not let them stop the church's progress. Most churches are in the condition that we see because that little problem in the church became the focus of the ministry. They took the focus off the promise that God had and that issue was only a distraction to the corporate body. Then, the distraction begins to affect individuals and now you're wondering why is your thinking all messed up?

Why are people leaving the church? It's because you took your focus off of what God originally gave you. Some people want the pastor involved in every little issue that is taking place within the ministry. No, the pastor doesn't have to be in that mess. He or she appoints leaders in the church to troubleshoot issues that take place while he or she stays focused on moving forward. Somebody's got to stand up there, keep guiding the ship and not cater to every little thing that's going on. So these imperfections have killed the church; they have kept us behind when we should have been ahead. Every problem is not your job to solve.

So, she's got leprosy and 3.5 million people have to stop for seven days. Think of the church as a plane. The saints are the passengers on the plane and the pastor is the pilot. When situations occur on the plane, we've got to learn how to how fix it while we are in the air. There is nowhere to land right now. We don't need a landing strip. We need to learn how to fix it in the air. The pilot doesn't need to come out of the cockpit. We need to learn how to fix it in the air. I don't care if an engine goes out, don't let the man or woman of God get out of the cockpit. Somebody crawl out on the wing, fix the engine and just keep on flying. Tell yourself, "We must reach our destination because someone must enter into rest and it might as well be us." It's not that no one cares about a person's individual difficulties; we just have a designated group to handle that designated situation, but we have to keep on flying. We can't come down now. We have to change it out while we are in the air. We're already up to 40,000 feet. Let's just change it while we are in the air. We have time to change it. We've been doing this a long time.

Listen, you're going to have Miriams; you're going to have Sanballat; you're going to have Gesham; you are going to have those type of people all the time. That is just a part of doing ministry. Moses had them; you're going to have them. Jesus had them; you're going to have them. You cannot get distracted when you have that kind of thing going on. Don't give it all the attention because you're putting too much energy into the wrong thing, and that's why you are not making any progress. So, we must stay in flight. When you stay in flight, you're going to make it.

DON'T CANCEL YOUR PROMISE

Never let internal imperfections cancel your promise. I am talking to the Body of Christ right now. Never let internal imperfections cancel your promise because every church is going to have some internal imperfections as long as there are people in the church. Don't let imperfections cancel out your promise. Don't land short of your destiny. You have enough fuel to make it. I used to think, "Well, God, maybe you want me to start and someone else finish, and I don't have a problem with that at all."

Then the Holy Spirit said, "No, I don't think so. You're the one who's finishing; you're not the one who's started, so you're going to see what I'm saying." I want to make an announcement to the church body, you are going to see what I've been saying throughout this book manifest in this season. Everything you say during this unprecedented season of peace, favor and abundance, we are going to see it, too. Like I've said before, when God blesses one of us, He blesses all of us. We don't want God to bless you without us, but when God blesses us, God blesses you and every need is met. I like what happened in the book of Acts. God said they had all things in common. Nobody was sick and nobody was broke. I like when Moses led them out of Egypt. The scripture records that "there was none feeble among them." When God really brings you out, He has the intentions of taking you in to something better.

Listen here, Susie who needs government help is about to come off assistance. You want to know why? Because we're a corporate body of believers and we aren't going to stop anywhere short of getting you to your destination. You are going to be the first of your generation, your bloodline, to enter into the promise that God has for you and nothing is going to stop you. God allowed you to read this book so you can reach your destination.

I got the plane metaphor while I was on a plane headed to South Africa. They said the flight would take fifteen hours. I've flown to other places, like Georgia and California, but those trips didn't take fifteen hours. So, if it takes fifteen hours to fly there, it means that there's more fuel in that plane than the one that I need to go to California, correct? Well, I want to tell you that you are on a bigger plane with more fuel and you are going to reach your destination. On the way back, as we were in mid-flight, someone on the plane got sick. I heard them come over the PA system and say, "Is there a doctor on board?" I was trying to sleep but I can't sleep when I hear about someone who needs help, especially in the area of sickness. (I've always catered to people who are sick.) I stayed in my seat since I'm not a licensed physician, but I start praying. I'm praying while we are in the middle of flying over the ocean and hours from landing in order to get to a hospital. So I just pray. I know the lady was really sick because I saw them bring her up front from coach to business class where she would have more comfort. Here's the praise report: the lady didn't die. They "fixed" it while we were in the air and got her to a place where she was healthy enough to walk on her own. They fixed some things while we were in flight. Fifteen hours of flying and she made it all the way to the United States of America. I don't know who this is for but some of you thought you were going to die in flight. There is no way on this type of structure (the Body of Christ), on this type of promise that you can die in flight.

God said to Joshua, "If they had entered in, He would not have spoken of another day." So if Joshua had it, why did God keep talking about it? If we have it, why does God keep sending this message to us that there is still a rest that remains? Whatever you have achieved is not rest, but there is a rest for you and it's not Heaven. I want to just mess up your theology that says "things are going to get better on the other side." Things get better on this side before I go to that side, and I want to make an announcement to you. I don't know how much you study your Bible. I don't know how much people watch Christian television but based on what I'm hearing, this is one of the best seasons of our Christian life that we have ever entered into. I've been looking for this season for a long time because I've been looking at my gauges, and my gauges hadn't been looking the way I wanted them to look. Now I can see in the distance. They say you can't see when you're flying, but I can see it with my spiritual eyes.

There is something about to flip in the Body of Christ to where we're no longer going to be looked at like we've been looked at in the past. You'd better get ready for restoration that you thought would never happen. I'm going to put everything on the line in faith in this season of my life, and that's why I'm operating the way I'm operating because I'm not coming down now. No, I'm like Nehemiah—you can say what you want to say, you can try to confuse everything, but I am not coming down. You need to announce in the atmosphere that you're not coming down; you're not going to be distracted; you're too high now; you're too far now; you've prayed too long; you've believed too much; you worshipped too deep; you can't come down now. It's not the time to land. This is the time to go higher into the higher dimensions of the things of God. See, listen, don't come down, I don't care what you've been experiencing, don't come down.

Years ago, I had an experience where I felt like I was being overwhelmed. And the Holy Spirit spoke to me while I was riding in my car and said, "Lift your head above the waters." It wasn't that the waters were overwhelming me; I just came down. When you feel overwhelmed, it's because you came down, not because the waters came up. Whenever you come down to that place called carnal, you're going to feel overwhelmed. Before I could get to the top of the hill in my car, I was feeling better because one Word from God helped me to get my head above the water. I don't care what's around my shoulders; I can still live, but I've got to keep my head; I've got to stay positive; I've got to stay in rejoicing. So from that day, every time I feel overwhelmed, it's a sign to me that the waters are reaching a place that they were never supposed to reach. I don't swim underwater; I swim on top of the water. In fact, this next dimension is water walking time. You will see what I'm saying manifest itself; remember, there were eleven men in that boat watching Peter walk. There's some stuff you were sinking in that you're about to walk on, and if everybody around you wants to stay pitiful, you need to find you another set of friends. In this season, your friends should stimulate you to go forward, not backward.

One time, my spiritual father, Bishop Eddie L. Long, called me and said, "When are you going to stop playing Little League?" I understood that he was telling me to come up to another level in how I operated. So, I want to say to you, "When are you going to stop playing Little League and start fighting the devil? Start telling the devil what to do." In Little League, you fight with the devil; in the Major Leagues, you tell the devil what to do. I believe that somebody's getting an upgrade as they read this book. You're going to stop wrestling and fighting with stuff, and you're going to start speaking to things. When you speak to things, they're going to come into alignment with what you said. I told Bishop Long, "I got you." See, he wasn't trying to insult me; he was stimulating something inside of me. It stimulated who I am. I want his words to stimulate you, too. It's time out for you to play around with those bills, trying to figure out how the ends are going to meet. The ends are overlapping in this season. You're not trying to figure out how you're going to pay your bills; you're trying to figure out whom God's telling you to sow into in this next season of your life. I want to change your thinking. You're not a beggar; you're a lender. You lend to nations; you've already shifted over into the higher place. I'm not walking around, trying to figure out what somebody's going to give me. I'm walking around trying to figure out what I'm going to give to somebody else. You're shifting right now; you're shifting into that place of the promise. You are a resource. I said, you are a resource. Stay in flight. All things are working together for your good. You love the Lord, and you are the called according to His purpose. It's working for you; just go higher.

FINAL DECREE

I declare and decree over everyone who reads this book success in every area. I declare and decree that God is now lifting you from where you were to where He wants you to be. I declare and decree this day that they are in a better place because you have used me to serve them through the message within these pages. I declare and decree that God would do tremendous things in your life. I declare and decree that you walk in unprecedented peace, favor and abundance. Amen, Amen and Amen.